PRAISE FOR *MY FLUORESCENT GOD*

Joe Guppy shows us what it is like to be a patient in a psychiatric unit and gives a three-dimensional and memorable portrait of the staff and patients he encounters there. This book is about suffering and confusion but it is far more than that. Guppy writes with quiet humor and grace and thereby transforms a painful time in his life into a story that we can all participate in and learn from, and even genuinely enjoy along the way. Moving and artful.

—*Steen Halling, PhD, Seattle University, author of*
Intimacy, Transcendence, and Psychology

I love this book because Joe Guppy's story is fascinating, and his writing is vivid and engaging. At the same time, I hate that this happened to him and could happen to anyone. A compelling read.

—*Lynne M. Baab, author of*
The Power of Listening

Joe Guppy describes the isolated experience of insanity with such insight, brilliance, and intensity, I found myself thinking, "Oh my god, this is exactly the hell of mental illness. I get it. I get it." Plus, it's often FUNNY. Not an easy task.

—*Lauren Weedman, author of*
A Woman Trapped in a Woman's Body

As an urban pastor, I am often asked to help people navigate the murky waters of life, mental illness, and faith. Joe Guppy's astonishingly frank account of all three doesn't offer an easy answer, but it does bear witness to a light of hope that can break through dark places.

—*Dan Baumgartner, First Presbyterian Church*
of Hollywood (CA)

To Pat –
Thanks for discussing!!
"Check it out."
Joe Guppy

MY
FLUORESCENT
GOD

A psychotherapist confronts his most challenging case—
his own.

BY JOE GUPPY

Booktrope Editions
Seattle, WA
2014

Cover design by Tim Gabor

Journal entry photographs by Valerie Vozza

Author photograph by Ernie Sapiro

Cover image copyright ©2014 by Joe Guppy

1980 photograph by William J. Murray III

PRINT ISBN 978-1-62015-441-0

EPUB ISBN 978-1-62015-451-9

Library of Congress Control Number: 2014912378

Dedicated to the memory of Steven Jesse Bernstein, who taught me that any experience can be written about; Dr. Jan Rowe, who taught me that any experience can be listened to; "Ma Dorothy" Guppy; Bill Guppy; and Ed Guppy.

CONTENTS

PART III POCKETS OF UNFINISHED BUSINESS: A CLINICAL REVIEW

(Current-day dialogues between the author and other counseling professionals)

A photograph of the copper owl rubbing I made at Seattle's Providence hospital in 1979.

INTRODUCTION

The taped-up cardboard box marked "Crazy Period" moved around with me for almost 30 years. I shoved it into closets in the bachelor pads of my mid-twenties and the apartment my wife and I shared as newlyweds. The box gathered dust for four years in Los Angeles and then in our two Seattle houses. I finally unsealed it after we downsized to a condo in 2007.

Inside were archives from my six months as a 23-year-old mental health patient in 1979: the daily psychiatric notes from my time in the hospital, my journals, my mother's journal, letters from friends, a copper rubbing of an owl from art therapy group, my grandmother's wooden rosary, plus old cassette tapes of interviews with my psychiatrist, psychiatric nurse, fellow patients, and the security guard who stopped me on the way to killing myself.

This book has three parts. The first two are my first-person narrative of the events of 1979. The third part features dialogues in which I discuss the case from my current-day perspective as a psychotherapist with my clinical colleagues, 30 years later.

The incidents in this memoir are true to my memories, as well as to my recollections as prompted by my archive materials and current-day interviews with some of the people who were there. On some occasions, I have combined characters, slightly altered chronology, and changed names and details to make a more readable narrative and to protect privacy.

PART I
INSTITUTIONALIZED

ONE

JUMPING-OFF PLACE

"Who's the president of the United States?"

"Jimmy Carter," I say flatly.

The psychiatrist peers at me through owl-eyed spectacles. We're seated across from each other in a narrow room in a large Seattle hospital. He masks his receding hairline with a comb-over. He wears a brown three-piece suit, white shirt, tie, and polished black dress shoes. His cuff is pressed into a blade. I think he might be Satan.

He nods and makes a checkmark on his clipboard. I sense his disdain and the vast chasm between who I was and who I am. I was a *summa cum laude* journalism student who, at age 21, landed a full-time summer job as a reporter for the *Seattle Times*. I thought I was hot stuff. Now, at 23, I am a crazy person.

"Count backwards from 100 by sevens," he says.

If he is Satan, then that proves this is Hell. Therefore, this mind-bending command must be the start of the mental torture.

I slowly grind out the subtractions until he tells me to stop.

I'm also working hard not to tell him about my plan to leap off the Aurora Bridge, a huge span a few miles north of the hospital. It's the nation's second most popular suicide spot, after San Francisco's Golden Gate.

Now he's asking me what year it is.

"1979."

My answer forces its way up through the colliding thoughts in my brain:

Kill myself. Died and sent to Hell. God. Punishment. Radioactive orange urine. Laurie, the Love of My Life. Betrayal. Mom. Dad. Torture. Pills. Horror. The starving children. And now the screaming starts.

Dr. Hardaway switches to asking personal questions in his robotic tone. I offer him a two-sentence version of my breakup with Laurie. I say something about God.

He's asking whether I want to kill myself. I struggle to call up the energy to lie, but I can't. I tell him my jumping plan.

The patient is distraught, anxious and occasionally trembling. He is guarded and suspicious. Has suicidal thoughts—jumping off Aurora Bridge. Fears hell. Despondency, hopelessness, mind racing.

—Psychiatrist's intake note, January 28, 1979

A year prior to my admission to the Providence Hospital mental ward, I was sitting on the toilet in my girlfriend Laurie's apartment re-reading "The Myth of Sisyphus" by Albert Camus. Laurie and I were proud to be the kind of couple who kept essays on French philosophy on the back of the toilet for casual bathroom reading. When we were falling in love, we spoke French and read *New Yorker* cartoons to each other.

I considered Camus' claim that the first philosophical question is: "Why don't you commit suicide?" I smirked at the limited vision of my former hero. I recalled a moment four years earlier when, as a depressed teen, I had gazed off into The Void from an 11th story balcony, just as Camus and Sartre had instructed me, and made the shrugging existential decision to not jump.

I'm way beyond that nonsense, I thought.

I had finally matured spiritually. I had rejected the barbaric Catholic God of my childhood and had moved beyond the dramatic angst of my teenage atheism. With Laurie, I had embraced the Tao and Zen, cobbling together from books a mixture of westernized eastern thought. Laurie and I wrote poems to each other imitating *The Way of Life* by Lao Tzu. One magic night, we met in a shared dream and held hands under the spreading arms of a maple tree.

Laurie was the most wondrous girl I had ever dated. I thought our honeymoon phase would never end. But we were hitting a rough patch.

Recently, we'd started throwing the I Ching, using three coins and a text with an introduction by Carl Jung. I was certain that following the synchronous guidance of ancient Chinese wisdom would re-birth our quantum connection within the collective unconscious.

Back at the mental ward, Dr. Hardaway doesn't look up from his clipboard when I start talking about my breakup with Laurie and sin and God and His punishments. He cuts off my ramblings and announces it's time for a physical exam. I meekly comply, but as Satan comes at me with his stethoscope, I'm terrified this is the start of the physical torture.

Dr. Hardaway concludes his assessment and hands me back to my parents. We are now in the waiting room for the hospital's two mental wards, which take up the entire second floor of the building.

My father stands up and walks with a disjointed gait to the window and stares out. He's gazing off in the direction of Seattle University, a Jesuit school one half mile away, where he taught psychology for 20 years and where he is now chief academic officer. Unlike me, he has always embodied calm competence, but now he appears as I have never seen him: confused, disturbed, unable to fix his son's madness.

I worry they'll notice that he's insane, too, and capture him and my mother. This will be my fault.

A male nurse with a neatly trimmed beard and pressed white uniform comes to usher me into the ward. He introduces himself as Bob. My legs feel watery as I move forward and let him take my arm. We stand at the front desk for a moment as my parents fade away down the hall. I'm grateful they're making their escape. Bob steps behind the desk into the nurses' area and gets a thermometer in a glass container from a glaring shiny shelf filled with them. I consider making a run for it.

Instead I follow Bob down the ward's central corridor to my room, where I see two beds separated by a curtain. Above each bed, a blood-pressure cuff hangs from the wall. Next to each bed are a rolling hospital table and a visitor's chair. This doesn't seem right. It should be the real thing, a padded cell with straw on the floor, and a yellowing straitjacket with a chain dangling from a metal loop on the back.

Bob takes out the thermometer. I see it as a rectal torture device, but he places it under my tongue.

A nurse calls me out of my room into the hall. She's pushing a cart filled with meds. She's pretty and looks about the same age as me. She says her name is Grace.

Grace. Grace. God's grace saves damned souls, I think.

But this Grace has a sly grin, dark ringlets, and is ghastly pale. She says that Dr. Hardaway has prescribed a medicine called Haldol, which sounds to me like "Hell-doll."

I tell Grace I'm not sure I want the medicine. She smiles at me with evil expectancy and places it in my hand. As she watches me drink from her little paper cup, its folded sides rustle against my fingertips. The liquid has a metallic tang that clings to my tongue and the lights are too bright.

"You're on your way now," she says.

Soon I have a whining yellow headache, my neck is cramping, and my limbs tingle with restless tension.

It's several hours later. I've got to get out of here.

I've scoped out the entrance to the ward a few times and I find it confusing. There's no big locked door. There's no door at all, just a large opening out to the main corridor, which has a number of enticing green exit signs over various doorways. The nurses' station, however, sits right next to the entrance, guarding it.

But the nurses often don't seem to be paying much attention, poring over notes or chatting with each other toward the back. One time I walk by and there isn't a nurse in sight. I force myself to casually linger in the opening to the corridor. I take one step out, then two, and look around, like I'm sightseeing, but secretly eyeing those exit signs.

Suddenly, Bob is standing next to me.

"Going somewhere?" he asks.

"No, not really," I say. "Just looking around."

"We ask that patients stay behind the line here," he says.

"Oh. Sure," I say.

We step back in.

I'm pacing the ward's hallway. My mind conjures up an image that thrills and comforts me: I'm standing on the pale green metal railing of the Aurora Bridge, my right hand resting on a light pole. My feet crunch flaking paint. Dark water is far below.

I'm pissed that I didn't get out to the bridge over the weekend while I had my chance. Now I'm five miles away. I need a backup plan.

Six blocks west is the English language school where I was employed before I went insane last week. There's an open area on the tenth floor of the building, perfect for jumping. I picture myself poised in the big sliding window, my right hand resting on the frame, the dark sidewalk far below.

In group therapy that evening, the chairs are in a circle and the buzzing voices mix with the buzzing in my head. Grace is leading the group. I know I'm going crazier because I can hear people speaking words, but I can't pull the words into sentences. Half the patients puff on cigarettes, filling the room with clouds of gray smoke. My nose is soon plugged, my throat raw.

Group ends. I walk out of the meeting room and again pace the corridor. I see Grace and mumble to her that I can't stand the smoking. She gives me a placid look. The unfairness of the smoke is too much. It's time to leave and kill myself.

But escape doesn't seem possible. This deflates the hope created by my imagined death.

I walk to the back of the ward where it dead-ends at the restrooms. As the door swings shut behind me, the arm of the automatic closer makes a squishy sound like a cartoon demon voice. I sit on the toilet lid and contemplate the three-inch crack of open window, which lets in the refreshing January night air. I stand and stick my nose into the opening and breathe. A car passes along the street 15 feet below. I push my palms against the bottom of the window frame to get more air. It keeps going up and up.

This is too easy.

I climb up on the sill and slide out onto the narrow concrete ledge that juts out from the window.

Perched on the side of the wall like a gargoyle, I surveyed the scene. A fifteen-foot drop confronted me. Below, people walked along, cars scooted in & out of the emergency entrance. I wondered if they could see me.

—Journal entry, 1979

TWO

PSYCHOSIS

One week before I entered the hospital, sane but highly stressed, I was sitting at an outdoor café in Mexico City, writing in my journal about the noise and hassles of my trip here to seek work as an English teacher. A cab driver tried to rip me off. A little guy wanted to steal my glasses. Dogs are everywhere, barking and snarling. The banks are chaotic and the tellers are rude.

I look up and see a skinny Mexican boy heading toward my table, waving his withered right arm around. It's thin, brown, and bone-twisted, with an embryonic hand flopping at the end of it. His other hand holds his begging cup, into which other patrons drop pesos with hardly a glance. Dread tightens my gut.

Back home, begging from table to table at an outdoor restaurant would not be tolerated. We keep the freaks out of sight. The boy is another reminder of the awful poverty I've witnessed in Mexico, and I haven't even seen the slums. He also brings to mind horrible television images of African and Asian children: impossibly scrawny, bellies distended, flies dotting their lips and eyelids.

As he nears my table, the boy's big brown eyes meet mine. I look away as my coins clatter into his cup.

My Mexican hostess picks me up from the café in her loud American Chevrolet. Nina, exotic and sexy, was a student at the English language school in Seattle where I hold my current poor-paying job. We had a brief romance shortly after Laurie and I broke up for the final time. I get into the Chevy and she roars off, merging perilously with the other cars careening down the street.

Her English has deteriorated, but she's no longer eager to have me teach and correct her. I timidly reach over and touch her hand. She gives a snorting laugh and pulls her hand away, then leans on the horn as another driver tries to cut in. He rolls down his window, shakes his fist, and screams something at her in Spanish.

It's a dog eat dog world, I think.

What can one say about Mexico? It's different. It's loud. My stomach is upset. I ask myself: where is my God? You must learn to control your worry. Try not to wish dogs and people out of existence. It's not nice.

—Journal entry, Mexico City, January 1979

I spend my last night in Mexico in a fancy hotel near the airport. I'm seated alone at a table in a nice dining room. No crippled beggars in here. I smile tightly as the elderly, too-subservient waiter refills my water glass, a white linen cloth draped over his arm.

Back in my room, homesick, I call my mother. I tell her I've turned down the teaching job.

"It's under the table," I say. "I'd have to work illegally."

I don't tell Mom that *I* have been turned down by Nina. I don't tell Mom about the begging children. I don't tell Mom my stomach feels weird.

I pretend I'm just calling to report on the trip, but in my family no one ever pays long-distance rates for casual conversation. I can tell the tension in my voice is setting off her own worry machine so I cut it short.

I try praying. That doesn't work.

I try to sleep but ruminations won't let me:

Other American teachers work here illegally. I am such a paranoid wimp!

I lost the girl of my dreams. What was I thinking? That other lovers — like Nina — would save me?

I hate my weirdo housemates. But who else would have me?

Another stomach rumble. I'm sure it's just tension. But wait:

"Don't drink the water!"

My doctor voiced that cliché when I saw him just before I left on this trip. And I have rigorously obeyed. But —*oh shit!*— a fancy restaurant with white tablecloths and clinking ice falling from a pitcher seduced me into gulping it down all during dinner!

My last night here and I screwed up. Idiot!

In a panic, I pull out the two travel medications my doctor prescribed before I left and look at the labels.

What did he say?

One pill was for lower gastrointestinal distress and the other was for upper gastrointestinal distress.

I close my eyes and strain to do an inner inventory. I decide my distress is "upper."

Probably means I've got something more horrible than the standard traveler's stomach.

But which pill is which? Shit!

I remember that the one for upper distress says "may color urine" on the label. I quickly down a couple of pills.

As worries strangle each other in my brain, I descend into a ragged sleep.

On the plane ride back to Seattle, I cringe at every creak of the wings, the hum of the incoming oxygen, the desperate roar of the engines. I jump when the lights flicker. I've always been a nervous flier, but now terror builds. I try to ignore that I'm trapped thousands of feet above the hard ground below in an aluminum tube, suspended in nothingness. I frantically struggle to conjure up whatever theories of physics keep the plane in the air.

Why don't we plummet to Earth? Maybe the Wright Brothers were prophets, creating a new reality with their powerful minds. Maybe the conspiracy of faith of everyone on the plane keeps us aloft. I look around. People calmly reading comfort me, but those whose faces betray twitches of doubt disturb me. I close my eyes and try to envision tiny molecules of air flowing under the wings, willing them to be solid.

It's dark and cloudy as we begin our nighttime descent into the Seattle airport. My sigh of relief catches in my throat when I look out the window and I see that my city is being bombed. When the clouds part I see flashes of light as the bombs explode. My heart thumps. I peer down, straining, and make out glimpses of smoke and flames.

We land. I forget to look for bomb damage as I scan the concourse for my older brother, who's coming to pick me up. The air smells synthetically crisp, as if the whole world is air-conditioned.

My mom's huge blue car pulls up. My brother Ed greets me with a grunt. I put my bag in the trunk and get in. The heavy door seals with a hiss, and I sink into the passenger seat. My brother has always been the quiet type, and I'm glad he doesn't want to talk.

The giant car is Mom's response to a traffic accident a few years ago. I remember her in the hospital. She lay there weak and helpless, with broken ribs. The small import car my economy-minded father had bought was totaled in the accident. She replaced it with this used Cadillac.

During the ride into the city, my sight, vision, touch, and hearing overlap and merge. Everything is electric blue and crackling: the air, the well-worn leather seats, the music streaming from the car stereo. I hear the Dire Straits' song "Sultans of Swing" for the first time, and its crackling blue guitar solo cuts through my brain like a wire egg slicer.

We get to my parents' house at 2:00 in the morning. My brother leaves in his own car. My car is also parked here, a crummy brown Toyota. I decide I can't face my cold rental house and weirdo housemates and decide to spend the night at Mom and Dad's.

I leave my mom a note telling her I'm here and check myself into a corner bedroom on the second floor, my younger brother Paul's old room.

I can't sleep. I sit on the end of the bed and look out the window toward Volunteer Park, acres of green space a half block away. That was where Ed and I played on the ancient swing set, as big as an oil rig. That was where I played pickup soccer games after school in seventh grade. That was where I got stoned with my gang of high school friends in the early 1970s and joined the Beatles, Carlos Castaneda, and the Grateful Dead in the cosmic spiritual experiences of the times. One magical afternoon we discovered that if you hung in the crook of a tree just right, supporting yourself on your elbows, you could read the word "FLY" in the crisscrossing branches in front of you.

Tonight I realize that packs of wild dogs are gathering in the park and the right thing to do is to go there so that, snarling and leaping, they will tear me to pieces. But I don't have the courage to leave Mommy and Daddy's house.

Or maybe I'm already dead.

I go into the bathroom and get a twin-blade razor and cut at the fleshy part of my hand between my thumb and forefinger. With increasing pressure and panic I see that I cannot bleed. I *am* dead. I gouge deeper. Blood finally flows. I'm briefly comforted.

I lie awake on the bed, propped up on pillows, yearning for the courage to go and face the dogs. Finally, I doze.

I'm startled awake when the door opens with a click and a demon version of my mother, hunched, with an outstretched claw hand, enters the room. I gasp, then stifle the sound. The flesh of her face shows the shadows of her skull. A deep chill sweeps through my body. She croaks out something. I tell her I'll be down in a minute.

Both my parents are in the kitchen. Dad is making his breakfast.

"Good morning, Joseph," he says brightly.

A house rule: Don't talk to Dad before he's had his coffee. He's had his first cup.

Dad walks off and I lift the lid on the pan on the stove to see what he is cooking. I see a grotesquely misshapen wiener, a bloated Polish sausage, alien and twisted, split open, entrails spilling out, bubbling in the harsh fluorescent light. I let out a sound and put the lid back quickly.

In the past I've been stoned in my parents' presence, needing to "maintain." This is that times a thousand.

After several hours of this, I tell my mother I need to talk. We go upstairs to the study where my father sits, doing something responsible like paying bills. I sit on one end of the couch, which used to belong to my dead grandmother. She died when I was ten. If you sniff the upholstery, it still smells like her house. My mom sits on the other end.

This is the traditional place for the few "family meetings" we've had over the years, never involving the whole family, just the brother in trouble and my parents.

My father leans back against his chair and asks what I want to talk about.

"I've gone crazy," I say.

"What do you mean?" my mother asks, tensing up.

My father seems calm, but I can feel my mother's distress.

"Everything is weird," I say, not wanting to hurt her more.

My eyes go to a pair of scissors stuck in a decorative cup on the bookshelf. I start to think about the fact that crazy people are dangerous. What if I stabbed my parents with those scissors? That would be horrible! I wouldn't do that. But since I am obviously crazy, how can I be sure?

I forget about the scissors because my father is talking. He's saying we can call someone.

Soon we are pulling up in front of an outpatient mental health clinic on South Capitol Hill. From somewhere inside my confusion, I'm glad something is being done. As we walk up the pebbly concrete sidewalk, I look up and see that the building is constructed with a terrifying surrealistic geometry. Walls and sections impossibly overlap in shifting angles. It's painful to look at. Grinding, mechanical metal parts are chained and hanging randomly on the exterior.

We make our way through a narrow maze of humming yellow corridors as my head grinds with a humming yellow headache. I'm left alone in an office with a social worker. He shakes my hand and says his name is Mr. Wiener, like what Dad boiled up for breakfast. This seems to me like an impossible coincidence, a sign that I've passed into another dimension. Mr. Wiener has an enormous hooked beak, sunken cheeks, and he makes a loud gulping sound when he speaks that shakes the room. His Adam's apple careens up and down his loose turkey neck.

I tell Mr. Wiener I still think a lot about my old girlfriend, Laurie. I sob into the tissue he gives me. He looks at me kindly like things should be better now, but the way his eyes bug out and his skin wobbles makes me pray his face doesn't slip down the front of his skull.

Next I'm talking to a psychiatrist. He seems cold at first, then impatient, then angry when I don't say anything. I don't want to be locked up. After a while, disgusted, he orders me to Harborview, Seattle's largest public hospital, for a thorough examination.

At Harborview, my disorientation reaches a new level. With my shriveled parents on either side of me, I'm walking through a tube-like corridor, sloshing uphill through yellow quicksand. My legs are enormous concrete pillars anchored far below. The yellow air keeps granulating, collapsing in front of me.

Now I'm sitting way up on an exam table as swarms of nurses in paper blue coats run around below me. My headache shifts from yellow to blue. One of the nurses puts a cardboard thermometer under my tongue and it erupts with a blue crackle in my mouth. The nurse pulls it out, pretends to study it, then looks at me with a smirk. They ask me endless questions—do you know where you are, what's your name, have you taken any medications, what year is it, what's four plus seven?

Suddenly, one of the nurse-clowns comes bouncing in, her paper coat puffing around at her waist. She's carrying a big red book that flops around in her hands. She says they've found the answer! She seems so excited she's going to piss herself, or break into song. Everything has switched from blue back to yellow.

"It's toxic psychosis! It's the pills you took for your stomach!! It will wear off in a couple of days!!!"

But this amazing theory is coming from the same surreal demons who have been baffling me for hours. They are trying to fool me with this excuse, to keep me in suspense before the crushing truth is revealed: I am Dead and Damned.

Or maybe they are real medical professionals and they have concocted this fairy tale, figuring that if I believe I have been poisoned by stomach pills I will be fooled into having hope, although we all know that my mind has finally broken and I have plunged into irreversible madness.

Well-intentioned gambit or satanic ruse, I see right through their maneuvers.

I am released into my parents' custody.

I'm up early Saturday after almost no sleep. My father often sleeps late on weekends, but today he won't get up at all. I keep sneaking up the stairs and looking into my parents' bedroom. He sleeps with the door open. It's a large room and the king-size bed is way over in the corner, against the curtained window. I have to peer into the darkness to make out the lump of his body. In horror, I see he may have died overnight. It could have happened. How could I be sure? I take a couple of steps in and consider going over to him and checking. But he doesn't like to be awakened. He'd think it was some emergency and it's not. He's good in an emergency. I am not. Why doesn't he just roll over or let out a loud breath or something so I don't have to stand here and worry?

He probably is dead.

I stare at his lifeless body for a while.

I go back to my room and sit on the bed, staring out the window. The Aurora Bridge is out there, way out there. West a couple miles, then north a couple of miles. I run a mental film clip of me leaping off of it. I could start walking. It would take me a long time to get there, but what else am I doing?

I check on Dad several more times before he finally shows up downstairs alive and makes his coffee.

What can a crazy person do on a drizzly Saturday afternoon? How about a walk in the park with his dad?

My father agrees to go with me and puts on his raincoat. In real life, we would not do this. We'd both be too busy. We get a few yards into the park where the path splits and he asks me which way I want to go. I can't decide.

"Come on," he says and heads off to the right. He thinks I'm weak for not deciding.

As we get further into the park I see the walk is a mistake. The wild dogs, who promised to meet me the other night and settle things, are gathering. I see two of them, a black lab and a big brown mutt, a hundred yards off, heading slowly in our direction. They are trying to make it seem casual.

I tell Dad I'm tired of the walk.

"I want to turn around now," I say. He gives me an odd look, but he seems to know he must do whatever his crazy son wants. I hate the excuse "I'm tired" because it makes me even wimpier in his eyes. But I don't want to panic him about the dogs.

The two dogs are coming closer. I spot several others in the distance. The lab and the mutt lope in front of us, moving their heads close together. They are sending out mental messages to the other dogs nearby. The brown one has sharp teeth and hanging pink gums and a drooling tongue. I imagine him and his brothers snarling and ripping, and my father screaming, his arms flailing above his head, caught up in his shredded bloody raincoat. The lab moves into the path to cut us off, herding us to where the rest of the pack is.

The title of a horror movie I've never seen starts looping in my head: *And Now the Screaming Starts*. I try to ignore it and continue my escape plan.

"Let's go this way," I say, turning quickly, leaving the path, and cutting across the wet grass. I don't care how weird Dad thinks I am; I'm saving our lives. If we make it home he'll even be spared knowing he was in danger. We're heading away from our house now, but I've got a plan to circle around and throw them off the scent. It works, and they are left staring after us, even as more dogs gather, too late.

I could not bear to have my father die the death meant for me.

The next day, I'm no better. My parents take me in the big blue Cadillac to Providence Hospital, where I am examined by Dr. Hardaway, admitted, given Haldol, and end up on the ledge outside the bathroom window.

THREE

TWIST

*This young man was crawling from a window ledge when he
jumped to the ground a distance of about 12 feet and suffered
an inversion injury of his left ankle.*

—Physician's note, January 28, 1979

I leap.

I land hard and start limping up the sidewalk. For a few seconds, it feels great to be free. I am locked on my goal—suicide—and my steely determination makes everything clean and simple, like the plain moonlight that shines on the sidewalk at my feet.

My ankle twinges. I might not make it to my old work building. Then I spot the hospital's tall brick smokestack, looming against the night sky, a metal ladder silhouetted up its side. It looks like a set for a 1930s gangster movie. Maybe I can jump from there. I increase my pace in that direction.

But someone is talking to me.

"Hey, hey…"

I look around. A short security guard is coming up behind me. He's a clean-cut, perky fellow with sandy hair.

"Hey, there…" he says.

I try to run, but pain shoots up my ankle and at most I can limp a bit faster. He's talking to his radio. The radio squawks back. He keeps pace but doesn't get too close.

"Say, do you need some help?" he asks.

"No, I can kill myself all on my own," I say.

"My name's Mike," he says, coming alongside. "Where are you going?"

"Are you a cop?" I ask. "Do you have a gun?"

He tells me no.

"Too bad, because you could shoot me. Mercy killing."

Another security guard shows up. Now that he's got backup, Mike is brave enough to grab my arm. His grip is firm but gentle.

"Let's go back to the hospital," he says.

"Fuckfuckfuck," I say.

"It looks like you hurt your ankle."

I let him wheel me around.

"Fuckfuckfuckfuckfuck," I say.

He takes a peek at my hospital bracelet and starts calling me Joseph.

"They should take a look at that ankle, Joseph," he says.

"Fuck you, Mike," I say, but not in a harsh way.

We take a few more steps.

"I just want to kill myself," I say. "Those meds they gave me have really messed me up."

We walk into the hospital entrance. As Mike pushes the elevator button, he waves off the second guard. We go up in the elevator. My cursing and Mike's soothing tones echo inside our little metal box. I start talking about Hell and religion and God.

"Keep the faith," Mike says. "No matter what, God will always be there. He'll be there to look over your shoulder."

"Fuckfuckfuck," I say.

Grace's placid facade cracks when Mike and I walk into the ward. No one had noticed my departure. I like this small victory.

They put me to bed and Grace makes me drink another little paper cup of Haldol. She leaves and Mike sits with me. He pulls my quilt up under my chin, the quilt my mom dropped off for me that afternoon, a quilt I've had since childhood. It has medieval horsemen on it, on a field of burnt orange. I look down at it and the blue pigment in the quilt becomes liquid and slides through the design like a flowing river, filling in where it is supposed to be. The hallucination frightens me and fills me with wonder.

Mike sits with me as I fall into a drugged sleep, still cursing.

I am awakened in the middle of the night, put in a wheelchair, and sent crashing through a series of metal swinging doors, like a fun-house ride. Big hairy men bring out machines and X-ray my ankle, then wrap it with a splint. I am wheeled back to my room and interred again beneath my quilt.

I wake to the torture finally starting. Someone is trying to twist my head off my neck. But no one is here.

My head is torqued over all the way to the right. I pull it back to the left and look straight up at the ceiling. Then my neck muscles tighten and my head starts to twist around again. I discover I can resist and slow it, but the twist is inexorable. When it reaches the farthest possible point, my muscles painfully straining, my chin pointing back over my right shoulder, I can, through force of will, pull my head back to the left. I am granted a moment of relief and then my head begins its forced march back to the right.

I don't remember the neck twist stopping, but I'm waking up and it's not happening. I move my neck to the left, then to the right to make sure. A male nurse I've never met sits in a chair next to the bed.

He's looking at me, his face alternating between a gleeful smile and puckering lip movements. I lift my head and stare at him. I notice I'm making those same lip movements, because my mouth is parched. He sees that I see he's mocking me and he exaggerates his imitation, twisting his lips ridiculously and making sucking sounds. There is a cup of water on the rolling hospital table between us, and I see something floating toward it. It's my hand. The hand grasps the cup with its fingers, bringing the straw to my lips.

I suck the water. The grains of ice rattle. The nurse's face laughs.

Patient appears very frightened, put to bed… All limbs shaking and hyperventilating.

—Nurse's note, January 1979

The spells, the shakes and the barking like a dog. Ahh. Ahh. Ahh.

—Journal entry, 1979

I rise to semiconsciousness in a different room. I am in a bed that is centered under a dim, rectangular fluorescent light affixed to a high ceiling. The walls are shadowy and dark red. One of my mental loops starts taunting me:

You made your bed, now lie in it.

There is the sound of rattling metal and someone is making an otherworldly barking sound. It's like a sharp staccato whimper, over and over and over. I am making that sound.

It is the sound of someone so frightened he doesn't want to make any noise but the terror must get out somehow. The rattling is me shaking the bed rails. I raise my upper body on my elbows and find that I am shackled to the bed frame by a thick leather belt around my waist. The barking changes to screaming.

People come in. I am thrashing and sweating. They roll me onto my side and hold me down. I am wearing nothing but my underwear. A hypodermic needle comes out. They pull my underwear down at the hip. There is no demonic laughter, just silent working. The needle jabs my butt muscle. I flinch and subside, then slide into darkness.

I wake and start thrashing and barking and screaming again. They swarm in with the needle for another round.

I come up out of a stupor and realize a nurse is sitting beside my bed. She looks like she's in her late thirties and has dull blonde curly hair. She says her name is Patricia. She has wide-set eyes, like an alien. They are blue and hold my attention. I start making the barking sound.

"Is that your choice—to do that?" she asks.

The question is abrupt and puzzles me and shuts me up.

Patricia says they'd like to try me without the "posey." That's what she calls the leather belt around my waist. She asks me if I think I can handle it. I don't know what she means, but if she's planning to free me, I'm all for it. I nod.

She produces a key and unlocks the belt. When Patricia leaves I get out of bed and explore. My ankle feels tender, but I can walk okay. The door is locked. The room is dark and quiet, but I can hear the muffled sounds of the hallway. I walk up to the blood red walls. My fingertips advance, floating before me, and then I am touching the nibs of medium-pile dark red carpet. I rub it, taking in the texture. I look down and see it meets the same type of carpet on the floor. A mental image of something dancing up and down the walls, like in a devilish Fred Astaire movie, floats past.

Who—or what—walks up and down the walls here?

Although I know that I have died and am in Hell, I also learn that I am in the security room: Room 262. Patricia comes in and tells me that, because of my jump out the window, I have been transferred from 2-North, where I was admitted, to the higher security ward down the hall, called 2-South.

The third night I am in Room 262, beginning to feel somewhat settled in my dark red cave, screams echo through the ward, waking me up. In the morning, Patricia tells me they need my room, and I am evicted.

I get to keep my bed. I accompany two nurses who roll it down the hall toward my new room. Wearing just a hospital gown and my underwear, I limp along on my sprained ankle. I reach out for the bed rail and help push a bit.

Patient presented himself in lounge with exaggerated trembling and sticking out of tongue… Patient was asked to stop shaking and to close his mouth and was able to do so.

—Nurse's note, February 1979

Now that I am back in a regular room, Patricia explains to me, I am expected to wear regular clothes. She lays them out on the bed and leaves. As I pull them on, I notice that my skin is sticky and my hair greasy. After screaming and sweating the past few days, I need a shower.

I don't want to call any attention to myself, but I screw up my courage and wander out into the hall and hesitantly tell a nurse that I think I might need a shower. She looks at me matter-of-factly and points to a door halfway down the hall.

I approach the door. Something doesn't look right. The door handle is too high off the floor. Maybe it's a trap. I look at the other doors up and down the corridor. Their handles are all the same—too high off the floor. I step in close and see that it measures as high as my hip.

With a start, I realize that standing here holding my hip next to the door handle is strange behavior. I quickly survey the corridor.

Whew. No one was watching.

I ease open the door and step inside. I'm on the lookout for demons or snakes that might be hiding in here, but the shower appears to be empty and safe. The stack of towels looks pretty standard. I'm nervous about the dark, hard corners and the necessity that I be naked, but I crave the normality of being clean. I cautiously place my clothes on a beige plastic bench and step into the shower. At first the water attacks my skin like a thousand electric needles, but soon it feels normal.

I fumble for the shampoo, squirt some into my hand, and palm it onto my head. I discover, with increasing panic, that although I can put my fingertips on my scalp and move them, I can't apply any pressure. I try with all my will... Nothing. I stare at my fingers and wiggle them. I'm not paralyzed. My muscles work. I try again to press my fingertips against my skull. I cannot apply pressure.

Impossible. Insane. Humiliating. Bizarre. Proof that I am living in an Alternate Dimension.

I rinse off the shampoo. My hair is still greasy.

I look down at my body. Something isn't right. Water droplets are bouncing off my legs. Some of them catch the light like rainbow orbs. They look too much like little marbles to be fully liquid. And I'm not sure they are bouncing correctly. The angles are off. They are moving too fast. It's chaos.

What are the physics of this parallel hell-world? Is this place ruled by quantum uncertainty or by Newton's laws? If the droplets are balls, is their movement predestined like Hume's billiard balls?

I want neither the rigid, predetermined slavery of Newton, Calvin, and B.F. Skinner nor the absurd godless chaos of Nietzsche, Vonnegut, and Camus. What a horrible choice! If choice even exists.

Where is God?

I dry myself hurriedly, creep back to my room, and go to bed.

I've read constantly since I was a kid. Now, when I hold a magazine up to my face, the text is a blur. Dr. Hardaway tells me blurred vision is a side effect of the medication. But I formulate a theory that he and his henchmen have decided to take away my eyesight before the screaming starts.

A few days later, I pick up a magazine and the print swims into focus. I panic when I discover that I can make out the words, but I can't follow them into meaningful sentences. And I can't "get" cartoons. They have printed a magazine that looks exactly like the *New Yorker*, but the articles make no sense and the cartoons are not jokes. It's not that I smile weakly at the cartoons because I don't feel up to laughing. They are nothing but weird pictures with disconnected words.

Humor has always been an important part of my life and identity. How can they have taken away that part of my brain? One of my happiest family memories is all of us watching comedy shows like *Get Smart* and *Monty Python*. It was great to laugh together, especially with my father.

I'd be afraid to see those shows now.

I am now allowed to go off the ward accompanied by a nurse. Patricia takes me up to the fourth floor to play the piano. I can poke at the keys but can't coordinate my hands.

There's a Ping-Pong table in the wide corridor that joins 2-North with 2-South. A muscular nurse named Terry takes some of us there to play. I'm excited because I'm a good Ping-Pong player. With my first clumsy serve, I see they have taken this away, too. I am infuriated by Terry's condescending encouragement. I am a phantom in a shadow play. Terry is a moderately good player, an obnoxious jock I would have relished destroying in Ping-Pong, knowing that he could kick my ass at football, running, weightlifting—or he could simply kick my ass.

Ping-Pong is running late and we have to get to the day room for lunch.

"Come on, everyone," Terry commands us. "Let's beat feet."

His gait takes on a strange wobble and he slaps his own butt.

This can't be happening. I've never heard the phrase "beat feet" before and I can't take it in. Something about a beating, someone's going to be beaten. Someone's feet will be beaten.

Terry is no longer a dumb jock. I remember I am dead and in a world of disguised monsters.

Most of the staff are not to be trusted, but Patricia and Melba might be okay. Patricia hassles me constantly, but she doesn't try to trick me or play mind games.

For several days running Patricia makes it her mission to get me to tell her how I got here. At first I won't talk, but she insists. It's all a jumble, but finally I piece together the tale of the trip to Mexico, the pills, the exam at Harborview, the crazy weekend at my parents' house, going crazier and crazier the whole time.

Since Dr. Hardaway and most of the other nurses seem suspicious of everything I say, I look at Patricia and brave the question:

"Does that sound okay to you?"

She seems to believe my story.

Melba is a kindly black nurse in her mid-fifties. She expects me to help make my bed and, working slowly alongside her, I sometimes briefly feel like an ordinary person doing an ordinary thing.

I mention to her one of my many regrets.

"I just wish I had never gone to Mexico," I say.

"Honey, there's no use crying over spilt milk," Melba says.

She delivers this tired cliché with such conviction that it's as if I've never heard it before. She's right! There *is* no use crying over spilt milk.

I just wish I could stop doing it.

Patricia persuades me to try one of the group activities called "Occupational Therapy." This sounds like we'll be stuffing envelopes, but it turns out to be more like fourth-grade arts and crafts. We meet in a large room off the corridor between 2-North and 2-South. Mandy, the group leader, is pretty, pony-tailed, and ridiculously upbeat and patient, refusing to concede an ounce of her cheerfulness to the droolings, starings, and fumblings of her charges.

"Today we're making Snickerdoodles!" she chirps.

I am angry at the dry, pale yellow cookies we produce. My family cookie is oatmeal chocolate chip. My mom, my brother Paul, and I can all whip up a batch at a moment's notice. Here, Mandy calls the shots.

A few days later, we try macramé. I'm sure I couldn't do it under the best conditions, but in any case my hands don't work. The next time, we make copper rubbings, which only requires that I clutch a square block and rub it back and forth over a piece of metal. I can't get much pressure, but I come up with a pretty decent image of an owl.

"What did you do in O.T. yesterday?" Patricia asks.

I show her my owl rubbing. She praises my efforts. Then she starts hassling me about getting up earlier, about making my bed, and about my "grooming and appearance." I feel too humiliated to tell Patricia I haven't been able to wash my hair.

Finally, I go up to Larry, one of the male nurses who seems like he might be an okay guy. He's shorter than me, with dark tousled hair. Quietly, with my head down, I tell him my problem. He goes with me to the shower room. I shower, and, when I'm ready, he wheels in a rolling white plastic chair with holes in it for the water to run through. I sit in it like an elderly or crippled person, naked in front of this other man. He comes around and stands behind me and washes my hair. He's good at using the hose showerhead without getting himself wet.

"It's a side effect of the meds," Larry says when we are done. "Be sure to tell us if you have any problem like this again."

Back in my room, I recall his kind hands and gentle voice and want to weep.

FOUR

FITTING IN

At 1:10 p.m. Joe was back. "I got inside the car and the walls were closing in." He also mentioned that his Dad was a bit upset... but Mom understood. We talked awhile.

—Nurse's note, February 1979

They might be poisoning my food, like in those murder mysteries where the victim is poisoned so slowly that he hardly notices as he fades away. I, too, can feel my powers ebbing away.

I venture into the day room and see a group of fellow patients playing cards. A woman introduces herself as Marie and invites me to join. She's about 40, with a soft smile and brown hair done up in a middle-aged housewife puffy hairdo.

I want to play. I also want to run around the table and shout:

"This is no time for games! We're prisoners! We've got to get out of here!"

But I'm not sure I can handle what's out there.

I pull up a chair. As we are about to start, I hear a voice behind me.

"Hey, Joe!" it says. "How's it going?"

I'm surprised to see Jimmy Gallagher, a guy from my neighborhood. We went to grade school together, but I haven't seen him in years. He's greeting me as if this is a chance meeting at the local tavern.

He sticks out a hand. I shake it weakly.

"I just got here," he says. "You been here long?"

"About a week," I say.

He's got a cleft in his chin and messy brown hair. In school, I always thought of him as one of the regular guys, someone who fit in. I remember enviously watching him, as he stood shirtless, at bat in a baseball game. Girls thought he was cute.

"I've been in and out of these places for the last couple of years," he says. "I was in Fairfax last time. If you ever have to go in again, try Fairfax."

Go in again? I think. *I just got here.*

Jimmy pulls up a chair. Marie deals.

I pick up my cards. In my previous life, I loved playing cards with friends. Marie starts explaining the game to me. Pinochle. We play several hands, but I can't grasp the rules. I get back to work on my theory that Dr. Hardaway is slowly removing pieces of my mind.

Jimmy leans over and points at a card in my hand, the next one I should play. I like that no one is getting mad at me.

The next day Jimmy ambles up as I'm hanging out in the corridor. He flashes his smile. He points to a woman patient with frizzy gray hair shuffling along.

"Her arms are at half-mast," he says.

The woman is holding her arms up at a 120-degree angle. I've seen other patients doing the same. She pauses and stares vacantly at me, like an extra from *Night of the Living Dead.*

"Too much Haldol," says Jimmy.

Will that happen to me? I think.

"Hey, are you getting shock treatment?" Jimmy asks.

"What? They do that?"

"Oh, yeah, they're very big on shock here," he says. "I'm not getting it but a lot are."

He gestures out at the ward.

A chill shoots through me. I remember Jack Nicholson strapped to the table in *Cuckoo's Nest.* I know about the forties film star Frances Farmer, given shock treatment, abused, and maybe even lobotomized at Western State Hospital. I think of Electro-Convulsive Therapy— ECT—as universally banned, last practiced by barbarian doctors who also doled out lobotomies in the fifties.

I hope Jimmy is pulling my rookie leg.

The next day, I sit down next to Marie in the lounge. She's playing solitaire. I make a suggestion for her next play.

"What brought you into this place?" she asks.

"I guess I'm nursing a broken heart," I say.

She seems kind and easy to talk to. I tell her about Laurie and also give her the official story that I overdosed on a travel medication.

"I've been depressed for years," she says. "Jimmy and I know each other from the hospital circuit."

Although the food may be poisoned, my captors are my only source of nourishment. Every day they put a paper menu on my tray so I can choose my meals for the next day. I get to circle the items I want with a stubby pencil. Cold cereal. Macaroni and cheese. Pudding. I never circle Jell-O.

It's Tuesday and the corridor is slowly filling up with the rolling beds of those given ECT. The patients lie there as they recover from the treatment. I start to walk past and am startled to see Marie in one of the beds. I look down.

She smiles weakly up at me.

"Hi, Joe," she says.

"Are you okay?"

"Yeah. But it gives me an excruciating headache."

Tears are streaming down her cheeks.

"Why do you let them do it?"

"It's the only thing that helps," she says.

I stand there a while and chat, keeping her company.

I call my mother in a panic.

"They do shock treatment here," I tell her.

"Dear," she says, "no one is talking about doing that to you."

She's getting that tone that tells me I'm worrying her with my crazy ideas.

I call my boss. I'm extremely nervous. Mom told me that he's the only one at work who knows which ward of the hospital I'm in—the nut ward. The others have been told I'm sick with a bad case of Montezuma's revenge. My boss assures me they are holding my job open. After I hang up, I brood for hours that I sounded weird on the phone.

My mother visits almost every day and often tells me that Dr. Hardaway says I am getting better.

"Don't you think you're getting better?" she asks.

"I don't know," I say, and look off.

I'm keeping secret my died-and-gone-to-Hell theory.

My cousin Joanna, who works in the hospital respiratory therapy department, also stops by often. Joanna is kind of a hippie. She wears Birkenstocks, often without socks, even during the winter. She's low-key and always has a smile for me, even when I'm feeling weird and acting odd.

After about a week and a half in the ward, my old friend Pete visits. I've known him since third grade. He joins a card game with Marie and Jimmy and me. Pete's presence makes me more aware of my condition. Just a few weeks ago, he knew my old self: active, quick-witted, sarcastic. On the basketball court he called me "Jumpin' Joe," and I called him "Pistol Pete." Now my humor has been removed and I am gaunt and scraggly, with a slow, hesitant walk.

When Joanna or Pete visits, I feel ashamed for them to see me like this. But I'm glad they bother to come and I admire their ability to act normal in this crazy place. Seeing them helps me cling to a tenuous hope that someday *I* may return to normal.

Everything I circle on the food menu invariably shows up the next day. They never get it wrong. I'm learning the cycle of meals and pick my favorites. Suspicions of poisoned food diminish.

My hand shakes as I sign myself out at the nurses' station for my first visit home. It's raining as Mom takes me out to the car. Dad's driving. Mom sits in the back and gestures that I get to have the front seat, like I'm a little kid. I don't want the front seat, but I get in and the heavy door closes with a clunk and a hiss.

My dad attempts pleasant conversation in his reserved way. We are driving north along 19th Avenue, toward the family home on Seattle's North Capitol Hill, a three-story house on a corner lot, which Dad bought for $22,000 in 1965. This purchase was one of my Depression-era dad's greatest victories. We got the house because in the 1960s, city homes were being abandoned for the suburbs. Sociologists called it "White Flight," but in my neighborhood it was "White Protestant Flight." The Protestants moved out and we Catholics moved in, centered around St. Joseph's, a white Gothic-style church. Most parents accepted the Catholic teaching on birth control, so hundreds of kids roamed the streets. With just six children, ours was a small family.

It's still raining as we approach Madison Street. I spot something up ahead that looks impossible. A line of gray wetness cuts precisely down the middle of the street, perfectly centered and extending east and west as far as I can see. On the other side of the line, the pavement is bone dry. As we pass over the line, the heavy rain hitting the windshield abruptly stops.

I am terror-struck. Rain doesn't have a clear border like that! I wake again to the fact that I'm in an alien dimension. I look over at my dad, if this man really is my dad.

"I need to go back to the hospital."

He flinches.

"What's the problem?" he asks.

"Take me back to the hospital!"

I can't look at him. I hear a sharp intake of breath from the back seat.

"Why?" Dad asks. "What's wrong?"

I can't say what's wrong. I am a loser and a weakling.

I start pounding on the dashboard.

"Take him back," Mom says. Dad turns the car around. I sense Dad's disgust and Mom's disappointment and fear.

When I was ten, my dad took my older brother and me camping and fishing at Lake Dorothy in the North Cascades. Dad jokingly claimed the lake was named after his mother. I was proud to be hiking along behind Dad and Ed with my small backpack. We slept outside in sleeping bags and ate out of metal World War II surplus mess kits.

In the morning we went fishing in the river that flowed out of Lake Dorothy and down the mountain. We moved among trees and rocks and brush. Everything was green, crisp, and clear. With Mom not there to worry, Dad allowed us to clamber along the boulders right next to a steep drop down to the river. At one point we were fishing in view of each other, but each of us had his own spot, each with a line in the water far below. I felt safe, basking in the calm beauty of the place and the confidence Dad had in me.

Back at the hospital after the aborted home visit, I punish myself relentlessly for my lack of courage. Obsessive phrases loop in my mind: *And now the screaming starts. You made your bed, now lie in it.*

A few days later, I am determined to complete a two-hour pass to my parents' house. I hang on for the car ride over, sometimes closing my eyes, forbidding myself to freak out. The house feels unnaturally frigid and the colors of the living-room rug glow strangely bright. I can't help noticing that all the doorknobs I measure against my hip are several inches below the ones in the hospital.

I get my lunch eaten, bite by bite, and make it safely back to the ward. *Whew.*

My doctor and my mother talk to me about transferring back to 2-North, the ward from which I escaped, for a program of intensive individual and group therapy. I fear I won't be able to handle the pressure, but I know that hanging out with the droolers and shufflers on 2-South does not match Mom's image of her boy.

On my elementary school report card, after the grades for reading, writing, geography, arithmetic, and so on, there were two statements followed by boxes for the teacher to check Yes or No.

Mine often went like this:

1) *Child is working to Grade Level: Yes*

2) *Child is working to Capacity: No*

I always felt angry and scared when I saw this, although at the time I wouldn't have had those words for the sinking, snarled-up feeling in my gut.

It's unfair. What more do you want from me? How much more?

In first grade, school was fun and I loved my teacher, a nice nun named Sister Michael Mary. On the progress chart on the classroom wall, my little yellow reading boat went whizzing around the blue construction paper lake. A plump kid with curly blonde hair was my only competition.

My reward for getting straight A's was an offer to skip second grade and go right into third grade the following year. My mom was proud, as was my budding ego.

I landed in the deep end of the third-grade pool, struggling to keep afloat amidst the demands of an unfriendly nun who was impervious to my charms. Eventually, I formed friendships with some of my new peers, but school was no fun again for a long time.

If you do well, they will demand that you do even more.

Jesus also demanded unending effort and could not be satisfied. If you had talents, you'd better multiply them or He'd throw you out into the darkness.

In fifth grade, the nuns made it clear what "eternal damnation" meant. My religion book said that those who fail to obey God are "tortured forever in Hell." In case you had any questions about what torture was, the section on the martyrs featured graphic drawings of Saint Lawrence roasting on a grill, Saint Sebastian pierced by arrows, others being stoned or flogged. Many of the boy and girl martyrs refused to let someone "touch them in an impure manner" and died horrible deaths, including one girl who declined a lesbian advance. This part of the book was creepy and titillating.

God was way up in the sky, looking down on us. He had His rulebook and His score sheet in front of Him, skeptically checking our behavior.

Jesus was no help at all. While on earth, Jesus seemed to hover a foot off the ground in His white robe, pitying the pathetic sinners around Him, who would eventually kill Him. At the end of the world, He would "return in glory" to take His revenge. A religion class picture showed a massive Jesus sitting in Last Judgment on a concrete-block chair. Like streams of ants, people were lined up at His feet, some trudging off to the left toward hell, some heading to the right toward heaven.

Early on I had perused sections of *The Rise and Fall of the Third Reich,* which loomed from our living-room bookshelf, a swastika beckoning from its spine. This not only deepened my tender young understanding of torture but also ingrained in me the image of the Nazi commandant who, with a wave of his hand, chose those prisoners who were to go to the gas chamber and those who were to be spared. I melded these images into "The Last Judgment by Giant Nazi Jesus on His Throne."

At the dreaded instant of my death, which could come at any time, I would startle awake in a panic and be face to face with Him and my Sins and Hell. My slim hope was a straining, incessant effort to be good.

The straining effort required of me today is the move to 2-North. I tell Marie I'm not sure I want to go. She encourages me to go for it.

It's Valentine's Day. Tomorrow I make the move. During her daily visit, my mother joins me in Occupational Therapy. Mom fashions a large red heart and skillfully lines it with lacy strips to make a valentine for my dad. I paste together a crude red and white assemblage for no one.

FIVE
Taking Responsibility

Patient said that he was down today because he got a card from his ex-girlfriend… Patient feels he is barely keeping a hold on some very uncomfortable feelings.

—Nurse's note, February 1979

Grace ushers me back into 2-North with a knowing grin that says:

"Now we get another shot at you."

I avoid her gaze. Roger greets me with an equally wily smile and hands me the 2-North program materials.

As I read about the program, the words and phrases set off bleeps of panic in my brain:

"Privileges and responsibilities—mandatory meetings—must meet criteria—show ability to control impulses—demonstrate significant progress—automatically revoked—"

I foresee a grinding cycle of failure, humiliation, and confusion.

But I perk up while reading the five-tier hierarchy of privileges:

1) Restricted.

2) Accompanied grounds.

3) Unaccompanied grounds.

4) Passes.

5) Discharge! (exclamation point mine)

Here's a game I can strive to win. But to earn privileges, I have to "Take Responsibility," a theme the staff brings up repeatedly, and which is reinforced by Dr. Hardaway. You have to take your medication, make your bed, interact in group, and "identify the problem." This last one is particularly vexing.

Sometimes this is my problem: I was upset over lots of issues, especially my breakup with Laurie, and then a toxic medication sent me over the edge.

Other times, it's this: Dr. Hardaway is secretly choreographing an elaborate conspiracy of mental, chemical, and physical punishments.

These two visions of reality slosh around in my psyche. At times they maintain an uneasy truce, other times they are violently at war, and at other times one perspective has the upper hand.

Dr. Hardaway keeps fiddling with my meds. He says different people respond differently to different medications and eventually he'll get the right mix. I imagine he sees my brain as a beaker, into which he pours different-colored bubbling liquids. I can't believe that peace or happiness comes through chemicals, and I wonder why no one seems to have found the right mix for the chronics. I worry I'll end up like one of them forever.

"Children are dying of hunger all over the world," I say to Dr. Hardaway, troubled by the matchstick-thin kids I saw on television in the day room.

He looks at me.

"What does that have to do with you?" he asks.

Dr. Hardaway constantly asks about my "suicidal thinking."

"What does it matter to you if I hurt myself?" I say.

Dr. Hardaway insists on referring to my jump out the window as a "suicide attempt." I explain that it was an escape attempt. I *did* want to go and kill myself, but I knew the drop from a second-story window wouldn't kill me.

I might be insane, but I'm not stupid.

One day I deliberately step on Dr. Hardaway's dress-shoe-encased foot to test my theory that he is a robot. I press as hard as I dare, trying to crunch his toes, but he doesn't react.

I miss Patricia and Melba. The nurses on 2-North are sophisticated psychiatric specialists, with an air of plastic friendliness. They look piercingly into my eyes. There is no such thing as a normal conversation. Anything I say is picked apart as "manipulative."

They call the patients "folks." They drop their *g*'s and sentences trail off to open-ended questions. A nurse might begin group with: "I was just wonderin' how folks are feelin' today…?"

Trouble is cooled with professional sympathy.

Exaggerated example:

A patient is strapped into bed, eyes bugging, thrashing, sweating, screaming.

Nurse: "Gee, I guess maybe things are feelin' kinda scary right now…?"

I can distinguish people on the ward by the pace of their gait. Patients shuffle. Nurses stroll. Psychiatrists stride.

Mom goes to the University of Washington medical library and brings back evidence for the "travel-medication-made-you-crazy" theory. She shows me a copy of a study conducted during World War II. The medicine is called Atabrine and was given to U.S. soldiers in tropical areas to prevent malaria. Two percent of the soldiers experienced some kind of disturbed mental reaction, although most effects were milder than mine and wore off in a few days. However, at the conclusion of the study, a couple of the soldiers hadn't yet recovered.

It's tempting to believe that's the problem, but I'm fearful that I would have gone crazy anyway and that the medicine really had no effect. I only took a few of the pills. I've been worried about Hell and damnation since fifth grade. I've always felt weird being so different from my father. And I definitely thought I was going insane the summer of my breakup with Laurie.

Dr. Hardaway doesn't seem to put much stock in the travel medication theory. I bet he thinks I'm just plain nuts.

One day I get up the nerve to ask Dr. Hardaway about some things that have been bothering me.

"Why is the ceiling so high in this little room? And the door handles are high, too."

I reach out and touch the door handle to show him how high it is.

"The ceilings are high in a hospital," he says, without looking up.

"Why is it that one of the elevators has two doors that slide apart but the other elevator has three doors that slide to the side?" I ask him.

"What is it inside you that makes you notice these things?" he asks back.

A chill shoots through me. I shut up.

The cuts I made on my hand with the razor prior to my admission have resolved to scabbed scratches. I show them to Dr. Hardaway.

"What do you think those are?" I ask.

"They look like cat scratches," he says.

Neither of us says anything more about it.

I'm starting to piece together the hidden connections.

"It's the pills," I say to Dr. Hardaway.

"Uh huh."

He's writing.

"The pills I took," I say. "They made my pee orange. The label on the pills said 'may color urine.'"

"Uh huh," he says.

I'm trying to approach an image in my mind that bothers me more than any other. It's not a memory picture, because I wasn't there, but it's something that really happened.

My old girlfriend, Laurie, waits alone, late at night, in the emergency room at the main Group Health building on Capitol Hill, about a half mile from her apartment. I picture her sitting on a bench against the yellow tile wall there amidst gray shadows thrown by dull lights. Her insides hurt. She couldn't take the fever and pain anymore so she walked up to the ER. She had wanted to call me for a ride, but:

"You told me not to call."

This loops and echoes in my brain.

Six weeks earlier, I had told Laurie we should take a break for a while. During our time apart, I slept with a couple of other girls as unstable as I was. I realized this was a huge mistake, and I desperately wanted to get back with Laurie. She was the love of my life; we belonged together. She agreed to meet with me at her place. When I finished begging and pleading my case, she told me about her late night trip to the ER.

"You told me not to call."

She wasn't trying to make me feel guilty or manipulate me to come back. That would have been better than what she *was* doing: calmly telling me why it was over.

I *had* told her not to call. She'd been calling me every day. How could I get some space when she kept calling?

"I couldn't call my best friend for help."

I was her best friend. I'd abandoned her.

She said she'd waited for hours at the ER. When she was finally examined, they told her she had a bladder infection. Probably "related to sexual intercourse." With me. Not a venereal disease—I hadn't yet broken our monogamy—but "related to sexual intercourse." After you have sex, they told her, you need to urinate right away.

They gave her some pills and told her to drink cranberry juice. She walked home alone and put herself to bed.

Laurie told me with a laugh that the bladder-infection pills "turned my pee bright radioactive orange." She was trying to lighten things up. But this only reminded me of the sense of humor we'd once shared, and everything else we would no longer share.

I had been there for the sex—for the pleasure—but when the pain drove her to the emergency room, I was nowhere to be found. For all I know, I was with another girl that night.

I tell Dr. Hardaway my big revelation:

"See, the label on *her* pill bottle also said 'may color urine.'"

My damnation is inescapable, but at least I'm figuring out how I got here and why I'm being punished.

I don't know what he's writing now.

I give up trying to explain to Dr. Hardaway the obvious connection. He can't read what I can—in black and white—the same warning on two pill bottles, mine and hers. God speaks in mysterious ways, in signs to be read by those who have eyes to see. And I can see that God has arranged my punishment with exquisite care and that I have died and am now in Hell, sent here through pills like those my girlfriend had to take because of my sin.

Dr. Hardaway cuts off the pill-bottle discussion. He says our time is over for today.

Left to my own devices, I lie in bed, grinding out some heavy theology.

I see that I'd be better off if I'd never heard of Jesus because people who are ignorant savages go floating off to limbo and aren't eligible for Hell.

You made your bed, now lie in it.

I realize that at your First Communion you are "granted eternal life," for better or for worse. I see a vision of myself as a foolish child, accepting the glowing white wafer of Christ, which slides down my throat and into my soul. Before ingestion, death would have obliterated me, but now I must live forever in either eternal bliss or eternal torment, and guess which one is for me?

And now the screaming starts.

But I must be taking some Responsibility, because I've worked my way up to Accompanied Grounds privileges. I sign up for a group field trip to the corner store right across from the hospital. I figure this tiny trip won't be any big deal, but when we start to cross the street, I panic inside. The air becomes unnaturally cold, the sunlight too harsh. I look down at my legs and force one foot in front of the other. The nurse and the other patients don't seem to notice.

The inside of the store is an explosion of color. Garish products lunge at me from the shelves like objects in a 3-D movie. I buy an Almond Joy.

I eat it back in the safety of the ward, a tasty memory of days long gone.

When I arrive for my next appointment with Dr. Hardaway, Susan, a slightly plump blonde nurse, is sitting in our small meeting room. Dr. Hardaway explains that he'd like Susan to stay—she's in training. I panic inside. I'm keeping a lot of thoughts hidden and concealing stuff from two people might be harder. I also don't want to talk in front of a cute girl my own age. Not so long ago I would have looked at Susan as someone not quite attractive enough for me to date, but I might have flirted with her. Now, as she looks at me, I feel neutered and humiliated.

"I don't think I want her to stay," I say.

Dr. Hardaway says nothing, but he seems exasperated. Susan picks up her clipboard and leaves.

As if we are physically sick, a nurse comes in every day to take each patient's pulse, blood pressure, and temperature. The next morning, as Susan is hooking up my blood-pressure cuff, I feel a twinge of guilt and try to make friendly conversation.

"You missed a real lively talk yesterday morning," I say to her jauntily. "Sorry I kicked you out."

She looks at me dubiously.

Since I live amongst a network of spies, Susan reports my comment to Dr. Hardaway.

"You personalize too much," he says. "You had every right to ask Susan to leave."

Then why did he seem so pissed off? I think.

"You shouldn't take responsibility for others' feelings," he says.

Dr. Hardaway gives me a book called *Your Perfect Right.* I read the first few pages. It's filled with painfully precise instructions and confusing, curlicue logic, just like the rest of the material from the therapy group.

I now have Unaccompanied Grounds privileges, which means I can go anywhere, as long as I don't leave the hospital's city block. In the morning, I can casually tell the staff to cancel my lunch and then go to the cafeteria and get anything I want, like a pile of mashed potatoes and gravy.

Even though it's out of my way, I like to use the hospital's grand central staircase. It's beautiful. Something from a bygone era. I imagine a debutante in a swooping gown, making her debut. There are four sets of stairs and four landings for each floor and wrought-iron railings with polished dark wood handrails smooth on my palm. I like to stand at the bottom and look up at the geometry of it, ascending grandly all the way to the top floor of the hospital. But the staircase does have one problem: At the very bottom is an extra turn with three extra stairs.

Weird. Why would they do that?

I ask Mom to bring me some of my favorite books from home. But I find out I can't follow fictional plots. My favorite history book bores me. The science book is filled with strange ideas. Even Harold and his purple crayon are too weird. I ask for a rosary and my mom brings me a cool black wooden one that used to belong to my dead grandmother. I can't remember all the prayers.

Mom brings me the mail she's been holding for me. Dr. Hardaway has decided I can handle the outside stimulation. I'm extremely anxious as I sit in my room, about to open the blue, gray, yellow, and red envelopes of all different sizes.

My mom is still telling people the cover story that I was hospitalized for a bad case of Montezuma's revenge. I get cards from friends, workmates, my housemates, and members of my comedy improvisation class. Only my boss knows I'm in a mental ward, and the others certainly don't know that my sense of humor has been wiped out by drugs and terror.

I read the wisecracks on the cartoonish get-well cards with mounting horror:

"What some people will do for attention!"

"What the hell Joe?"

"Save some Jell-O for me!"

"Dear Auntie Em, I promise I'll never go away again."

The humorous references are lost on me. I can't make the connections.

But the letter I've saved for last spells the end of my fledgling mental stability. It's a short, friendly get-well note from Laurie. It ends with: "I hope the enclosed cheers you up."

She's included a photo of me brushing my teeth, standing in front of the mirror in her bathroom. It's a full-body back view and I'm wearing a T-shirt, naked from the waist down. This cannot possibly be real. It must be a hallucination or a message from another dimension. Laurie doesn't know I'm in the loony bin, but still—there is no way she would send such an intimate photograph after all the heartache and drama of our breakup.

I want to keep my mail freak-out a secret, but this is too much.

When Mom visits in the afternoon, I show her the photo. I'm humiliated, but I know if I keep silent the last intact pieces of my mind will shatter. There is some relief in seeing that she sees what I see and that she, too, is shocked and outraged.

When Laurie and I broke up, I had complained to Mom that she had treated me unfairly, and my mother joined me in condemning her. Of course, I never told Mom about my infidelities, Laurie's trip to the ER, or anything else that was my fault.

Mom takes the letter and photo. She later tells me she destroyed them.

I am failing at all the assigned tasks on 2-North. I'm not taking responsibility or meeting expectations. The hardest work I do is trying to keep my theories secret. Pressure mounts with every weird thing I notice: the elevator doors, the door handles, God's punishment pills, the starving children, Dr. Hardaway's dead foot, the photo Laurie sent. Sometimes I feel like the molecules in my body are shaking apart. I get headaches that feel like an arid, empty space is expanding in my brain, pressing against my skull with a high whining sound.

The pressure is becoming too much.

I must do something.

SIX
RETAINED

Community meeting held in response to female patient acting out (breaking window)—Joe shared feelings and related his experience of feeling out of control when he was first on the unit.

—Nurse's note, February 1979

Less suspicious today—some increase in insight. Feels "empty—empty—empty." Feels that "love" would fill him up.

—Psychiatrist's note, February 1979

As Susan takes my blood pressure, I worry that my racing heartbeat reveals how crazy I am. I know they won't let me out of here unless they think I'm getting better. Susan hands me my pills. At best, Dr. Hardaway's chemicals are useless. At worst, they are Satan's potions. I swallow the pills, then go to the bathroom, stick a finger down my throat, and vomit them up.

The next morning when Susan gives me the meds, I hold them under my tongue while she hooks up the blood-pressure cuff. I wait silently for the procedure to be over, trying to will a normal heartbeat. When she leaves, I spit out the meds.

I do that for about a week. Nothing changes.

Then one morning Susan looks up from the blood-pressure cuff while I have the meds under my tongue. She seems to be giving me a funny look.

She knows. Damn it! Busted. Guilty.

I slowly open my mouth and show her. I give a little laugh, but it's muffled by the pills. Susan looks shocked and disappointed, like a nun from grade school discovering that Joseph isn't the good little boy she thought he was.

She didn't know!

Damn.

I show her the other capsules I've stashed behind my bed frame. They are wrinkled up in their plastic shells, like a row of dead insects. I don't know why I've been saving them.

I hope she doesn't get in trouble, I think.

Dr. Hardaway has this to say about my medication boycott:

"Sometimes when you miss your freeway exit it takes a long time to get back on the right road."

I feel hopeless panic rising, but I say nothing.

The next time I try to go to the cafeteria for lunch, I find I have been busted back down to Accompanied Grounds privileges.

In a day or so, I'm desperate enough to try a couple of things they're always wanting me to do: "socialize" and "get some exercise." The splint has been taken off my ankle, and I've been able to lightly trot up and down the ward. I ask a newer patient, Cliff, if he wants to go jogging with me. He has Unaccompanied Grounds so he can be my chaperone. He's only 19. When he was admitted I outranked him in privileges. Tables have turned.

We head off. Since the hospital occupies an entire city block, we're allowed to jog on the sidewalk but not to cross the street. The ankle feels pretty good. I start thinking about taking off in the direction of my old neighborhood. Freedom awaits and the Aurora Bridge hovers out there as a beacon of hope. I don't think Cliff would try to stop me.

I get distracted by the blobs of gum on the sidewalk. They whiz by under our feet: shades of dirty gray, dirty green, and dirty pink— all smashed into the concrete like elf turds.

How could so much gum come out of the mouths of so many? You never see anyone spit gum on the sidewalk.

As we round the corner and start down 18th Avenue, the gum-blob inventory plummets. I keep checking the sidewalk. There's hardly any gum!

I look over at Cliff, huffing and puffing beside me. He gives me a little head nod. I smile insincerely. The otherworld feeling is coming on strong. I hate it but it gives me a jolt of energy.

He leads us back to the ward. We leave behind the gum crisis and my chance to run off.

The therapists have implemented a change in the group therapy smoking policy. Now only one person can smoke at a time. The smokers fidget with their cigarettes in group until their lucky moment arrives.

I know that this is because of my complaining. They had to take me seriously because I jumped out the window. I feel a shameful and smirky power. I have this same feeling as I sit in the bathroom, looking up at the window I jumped out of. They've blocked it so it opens just a few inches.

But my brain has come up with a new secret escape plan I try not to think about.

I stare down at the floor tile. A darkened portion of grout forms an unmistakable cross. It's the cross of Christ, mocking me here in Hell. Or is it a message of hope, carved out just for me?

"My God, my God, why have you forsaken me?"

As I leave the bathroom, the automatic door closer squeaks sloppily in its grease. It sounds like someone talking, but I can't make out any words.

Nurses are constantly asking me:
"Do you hear voices?"
I say back to them:
"I hear your voice."
What I mean is:
Maybe your voice is a hallucination.
It could be. Didn't Descartes prove that?
"I think therefore I am."
My own thinking never ceases. Everything else could be a hallucination.

I keep it together a few more days and get Unaccompanied Grounds privileges back. I make an appointment for "pastoral care." I float up the big central staircase and appear like a hesitant ghost in the doorway of the chaplain's office. The chaplain, a Catholic priest, stands up at his desk and beckons me in. He's wearing the traditional pressed black suit with white-notched collar.

His name is Father Keyes. Keyes—Keys—He holds the Keys to the Kingdom.

The priest can make your sins stick to your soul, or he can wipe them clean. It's a power given to Peter by Jesus personally. The religion book picture showed Peter kneeling before Jesus, who places a magic hand on his shoulder, and says:

"Whose sins you will retain, they are retained."

I sit in the chair facing Father Keyes. I force myself to say that I'm afraid of Hell. He shifts in his chair and places his forearms on the desk. He clears his throat and says something.

I knew he wouldn't be able to offer any comfort. I know the teaching as well as he does. You have to wait until you face Giant Nazi Jesus and He waves you to the left or to the right. In a way I admire that the priest doesn't make excuses. Even though he knows I'm insane, he keeps his integrity and doesn't give me any phony assurances.

Every evening a recording of the 23rd Psalm is piped throughout the hospital. A sonorous male voice intones, "The Lord is my Shepherd, I shall not want... and though I may walk through the Valley of the Shadow of Death I shall fear no Evil..."

The voice seems to savor the words "shadow," "death," and "evil."

Although the treatment schedule is stifling and the staff play mind games, I am determined to participate so I can get out of here. One day, the group focuses on a woman patient who freaked out, ran screaming around the ward, and then broke a window with her fist. She sits in her chair, face drawn tight, hands clutched, as Roger describes her "acting out." I can feel her fear.

I raise my hand, even though you don't have to. I describe my first day here and my escape attempt. I talk about how "out of control" I was, using their jargon. Actually, when I went out the window I felt totally *in* control.

After I speak, my "willingness to be open" and "empathy" garner praise from Roger and Grace. I smile tightly and nod. I've learned that my "low self-esteem" leads me to be "unwilling to accept a compliment" so I try to take it in. But I still feel like a fake. While I was speaking, I felt a shaky coldness, and I could sense the phoniness puffing up in me until I was a stretched-thin balloon.

If you only knew how crazy I still am!

That night, in a family therapy meeting, my parents talk about how different I was before I went to Mexico. Dad calmly explains that I used to have a good sense of humor and a greater range of emotion. Dr. Hardaway nods but seems doubtful. I don't think he believes a word of it.

My jogging partner, Cliff, earns his way to Privilege Level Five and is discharged.

Dr. Hardaway surprises me by talking about discharge for me, maybe next week. But first I must pass a test: an overnight visit to my parents' house. And there's the "group decision-making process." I have to decide whether I want to go, and then the group votes on whether they think I'm ready. I resent that the group gets to decide my fate, but I hope they can help me make up my mind.

The conversation goes around in circles. If another patient starts to say something helpful, Grace intervenes with a warning about my "dependency on the group."

I fear if I don't go, I will be stuck here forever, but I'm terrified if I do go, I will freak out again. I finally blurt out that I want to go. The group approves.

My family has staged a normal dinner at home, as part of my overnight test. Two of my younger brothers are there, along with my mom and dad. It's still weirdly cold and the rug colors still glow. My dad's beer looks good, but I don't think I should drink because of the meds. I choose an orange soda, like a wimp.

We're having steak, a special treat for me. The great American luxury meal! We're using the steak knives Mom collected one by one at the Shell station up the street. Childhood memories flood in, leaving me floating on sadness. I know now that Mom always buys the cheap cuts, but, as kids, all we knew was: "IT'S STEAK!" She'd broil it in the oven, the rim of fat crackling. My dad would bring the manly steak sauce to the table.

But wait, there's something on the family table I've never seen before. It's like the *Sesame Street* song:

"One of these things just doesn't belong."

I'm looking at a plastic spice container marked "Janet's Krazy Mixed-Up Salt." It cannot possibly be real. I pick it up. It has a transparent bottom, so you can look up into it and see how Krazy and Mixed-Up it is. There are wacky colors on the label. It must be laced with LSD, and if my family consumes it, they will become as crazy as I am. I cannot let this happen.

Everyone is milling around. Finally, I have a chance to sneak the stuff off the table. I'm panicking that the seasoning might be missed, but I have to do the right thing. I pretend to go to the bathroom. I creep outside and toss Janet's Krazy Mixed-Up Salt into the garbage can. I return to the group, but then I start to worry someone will see it in the can. I slip out again and bury it deeper into the garbage.

We sit down to eat the steaks. Everyone seems so tense. I know it's my fault. But at least I saved them from the LSD salt.

After dinner, my younger brother Tim suggests that everyone go out to my dad's garage and look at some cool new thing he put in his car. I feel horrible because back on the normal planet I used to live on, I took Tim to a car show once. We saw lots of vintage autos, a fifties rock 'n' roll band, and we talked with Robin of the Batman TV show. I wrote a newspaper story about it. I used to be the hot-shot reporter and the cool older brother. I feel so guilty now that I'm not that guy anymore.

On the 15-foot walk from the house to the garage, I come to understand that I'm surrounded by demons who look like my family. They're taking me to the garage to torture me with my father's tools.

It was never going to happen at the hospital!

The crippling chill descends and the electric thrill ascends. My "brother" opens the door with a click. They have maneuvered themselves to block my escape. I meekly go in. The shop grease smell hits my nostrils.

And now the screaming starts.

But my brother just shows everyone his car.

That night, I lie in bed in my parents' house, not sleeping. It's the same bed I was not sleeping in weeks ago when this all began. I'm no better.

Then it hits me. I'll drive to Don and Vi's! Don and Vi are legendary old friends of my parents, who left city life and good jobs at Boeing and bought a bed and breakfast on the Oregon Coast in 1969. One of my fondest memories is of family vacations at Wavecrest, a magical old inn they furnished with antiques they'd collected from all over the world.

Don built a roaring fire every evening in the living room and we sat around reading and talking. They had no television. My favorite books of theirs were collections of old *New Yorker* and Charles Addams cartoons.

Don was a few years older than my father, and he had a beatnik goatee and white hair that swooped up the sides of his head. His eyes crinkled when he laughed. One morning, I got up before anyone else and joined Don in the kitchen, where he was baking bread. While the dough rose, we sat and talked. He actually seemed interested in my ideas and responded with ideas of his own. No adult had ever done this. Once, we walked down to the beach together and then stood there silently watching the waves.

I'm now convinced that Don and Vi's inn is a friendly place where I can sort things out. I tiptoe downstairs and find the extra key to my brother Ed's 1960 Volkswagen Bug. I slink out and walk about a mile to my brother's apartment. The Volks is right out front in Ed's parking spot. I get in, put it in neutral, and roll the car down the street so Ed won't hear the engine start. When I'm a half block away I fire it up.

On my way to Interstate 5, I stop and fill up the tank at an all-night station. Despite my father's knowledge of engines and the painless assimilation of this knowledge by every one of my brothers, I barely know anything about cars. But I can check the oil. I have a rag in one hand to wipe the dipstick, and I still have the gas cap in my other hand. As I reach for the dipstick, I drop the gas cap into the depths of the engine.

Shit.

I peer in but I can't see anything. Maybe the gas station attendant is getting suspicious or maybe even calling Satan. I walk to the side of the car, stuff the rag into the gas tank opening, and take off.

Just before I get onto the freeway I feel compelled to pull over and check my improvised gas cap. The rag has slipped almost all the way into the tank. I reach for it, and it falls into the abyss.

Fuckfuckfuckfuckfuck.

I can't do anything right. I just blew my last chance to do something on my own.

Goddamn it. You're an idiot.

My dad used to call me an idiot. Or maybe he only said it once.

When I was in college, a colleague of my dad's told me that my dad once said I was smart. I devoured the compliment like a starving dog.

I take Ed's car back to his apartment and park it in his spot. I walk back to my parents' house, re-hang the key, go to bed, don't sleep, and pretend everything's normal in the morning. My overnight pass is an apparent success.

Back at the hospital, all I can think about is my brother driving around with that rag in his gas tank. Could it clog things up somehow? Start a fire? Finally, I ask to use the phone, and I call my dad.

"Dad, I dropped a rag in Ed's gas tank."

"Sure. That's okay."

What? Why is he so calm? Does he know all about it already? What the heck is going on?

"Don't worry about it," he says. "We'll take care of it."

This can't be my dad. Dad would be pissed. Or ask questions. Or something.

"Okay, Dad," I say. We hang up.

At 3:00 in the morning I'm wide awake again. But I'm at peace. I have realized that since I'm in a completely unreal phantom world I have nothing to worry about. I could pass through the walls if I really wanted to. I see a clear vision of myself striding out of the hospital into the cartoon night, spreading my arms to the universe, and finding out what happens next in this grand adventure. Like maybe me finally jumping off the Aurora Bridge.

I walk out into the hall. As usual, one nurse is stationed at the front desk blocking the way out through the front entrance. Luckily, I have my secret plan.

Roger and one of his pals are pulling the all-night shift, camped out in the day room. I can tell by the way they glow that they are holograms. The TV is on. Roger eyes me suspiciously. I pacify him with some normal banter. They're surrounded by stacks of tabloid-style newspapers.

"What are you doing?" I ask.

"We're stuffing flyers," says Roger. He adds something about some organization he belongs to. I don't follow what he is saying.

"Can I help?"

"Sure."

We stuff flyers for a while. We're a team.

The TV starts running another one of those long CARE ads featuring African children with big eyes, swollen bellies, and brazen flies. I cannot comprehend such horrors, but at least they offer more proof that I live in an unreal world. The number comes on the screen and I tell Roger I want to use the phone and make a donation. I really do want to help the poor starving children. I have some money in the bank. He tells me I can't use the phone.

Okay.

It's time to leave. Here's my plan:

The front entrance is guarded and the back stairwell is locked. But there is an elevator down the hall—the one with three door panels— that opens up from time to time with staff bringing in laundry and stuff. When the guy leaves the ward, he just pushes the button and rolls his laundry cart into the elevator. There's no key or anything.

I bid Roger and his buddy goodnight and stroll casually down to the elevator. I push the button. It lights up nicely. I glance down the hall. All is quiet. Then I see Roger peeking his head out. Shit. That's ridiculous. How could he know I wasn't walking back to my room? Oh well, he's just a phantom.

He and his buddy are hauling ass in my direction as the elevator door opens. I hop in and push the first-floor button. The door starts to close. I jab at the "close door" button again and again.

The door is almost shut when Roger jams his arm in. The door retracts. The two phantoms jump in. Each of them grabs one of my arms. They start pushing me out. My feet stutter on the floor. I'm shocked that I can't pass through their phantom bodies by waving my hands. But they remain solid, bringing me inexorably back into the ward.

They give me more drugs and then haul me back to 2-South and security Room 262.

SEVEN

RESISTANCE

He began to delegate all his possessions to various family members. His eyes filled when I told him that he would be using his things himself. "I needed to hear that," he said. "OK, I can sleep now."

—Nurse's note, February 1979

In the morning, Patricia and Melba are with me. I'm sitting on the side of the bed, panting and sweating. My grandmother's black wooden rosary dangles onto the belly of my sweaty T-shirt.

"Please don't leave me alone," I say.

I squeeze their hands.

"You should drink something," Patricia says. She holds out a waxed hospital cup.

I look at her face. In an instant, the lighting becomes harsh and the dark red room darkens and reddens. Patricia now has gray half-moons under her eyes and pockmarks gouge her cheeks. I look again at her hand. The veins are purple and ropy. Melba shifts. Her uniform rustles loudly. The hum of the fluorescent light fills the room.

I shake my head at the cup.

I hear Patricia's voice.

"It's grapefruit juice."

"Does it have Haldol in it?"

"No."

"Are you sure?"

"It's just juice."

I take a sip. I don't taste the bitter tang of Haldol. But grapefruit juice is a pretty strong cover-up.

I look again at Patricia. She looks better. Sounds are back to normal. I drink the juice.

Patricia asks me if I'm feeling suicidal. I don't want to talk. She insists.

"Do you think suicide is wrong?" I ask. "I mean—shouldn't people have a right to do what they want with their own life?"

She looks steadily at me.

"You're intellectualizing. Do you feel suicidal?"

I say it would be okay if I died. I say I'm afraid I'm going to die soon. I say I'm afraid I will never be able to die. I say I'm afraid I've already died.

Melba chimes in. "Do you have thoughts of killing yourself?"

"I don't know how I could," I say.

This doesn't seem to satisfy them.

"Don't leave me," I say. I start panting. I'm afraid I'm going to be screaming soon.

They want me to get in the bed.

Okay.

Patricia brings out the posey, the leather belt that straps me to the bed frame.

"For your protection."

Okay.

She puts it around my waist and locks it. I drift off to sleep.

I'm not sure I'm dreaming. It's more like a dozing vision. I am descending a square staircase, like the main staircase in the hospital. But this staircase is all white. My head is consumed by a bitter, burnt-yellow, whining ache. Each flight of stairs is about eight steps. I descend one flight. I take a 45-degree turn and start down the next set of stairs. The pain in my head doubles.

This is such intense, pressured agony that a worse pain could not be conceived.

At the bottom of that flight, I mechanically quarter-turn again, start down the next flight, and the pain doubles again. At this level of pain, part of the brain is again convinced it cannot get worse, but another part, trapped in panic, now grasps the logic, the pattern. There is no escape. The next turn approaches. This pain will double and then double again. The staircase goes down forever. It doesn't lead to Hell. It is Hell.

When I wake up, Patricia is standing next to the bed.

I tell her, "I have terrible dreams—but then—maybe I'm not asleep at all."

I start listing my belongings and which family members should receive them. Patricia tells me I will need my things for myself.

Patricia asks me a lot about trust and suspicion. I tell her I think I can trust her and Melba. I don't trust Dr. Hardaway.

I shuffle into the day room and Marie welcomes me back to 2-South. She invites me into a card game. It's nice to see her and the others, but I feel stupid, having flunked out of 2-North.

Over the next couple of days, Patricia and I have some deep talks, mainly at her insistence.

"We need to get to the heart of what's bothering you," she says.

I tell her more about the breakup with Laurie. I confess that I feel guilty for betraying Laurie by sleeping with other girls when we were "on a break." I feel guilty for seducing the other women by pretending I was interested in them, when I was pretty much just interested in sex.

My sins deserve great punishment, I think.

"I don't want you to think of me as a terrible person," I say to Patricia. She says she doesn't.

Then I confess the humiliating secret that, when I was a teenager, I would raid this box of books on sex that my dad kept in a cardboard box on the floor of his study. They were for a human sexuality class he used to teach. I would take out a few choice items, then lock myself in the bathroom and masturbate. I felt even more ashamed of having searched through my brothers' dresser drawers and closets, looking for sexual material. I stress to Patricia that I never read anyone's private diaries. I just wanted to find the girlie magazines.

I fear she will be shocked, but Patricia says she understands. It makes sense that I felt badly about violating people's privacy, but my interest in sex and my desire to look at the magazines were normal. Her acceptance makes me feel less guilty, less in need of punishment.

I can't believe I'm talking to a woman about this stuff, I think, *but I am desperate.*

I write in my journal:

"Dear God,
I want so much to get out of here and into my usual self.
Hopefully, a better self. I want to be forgiven. I want to see
Father Carroll. Remember Michael's Dad's funeral. The
sermon was so good."

Just a few months before I went into the hospital, a high school classmate's father fell while working on the roof of his family home. He was killed. I didn't really know the dad, but I was shocked by my friend's loss. I went to the funeral at our neighborhood church, St. Joseph's. The place was packed. I felt numb, but the sermon by Father Patrick Carroll was uplifting. He talked about a gospel passage in which Jesus says, "Let not your hearts be troubled or afraid."

My heart is extremely troubled and afraid. I tell Mom I want to see Father Carroll.

As a child, I found Catholic Mass to be excruciatingly long and boring. But sometime in the 1970s, the "home Mass movement" was born. When Father Carroll said Mass over at my best friend's house, it lasted 30 minutes at most. Father Carroll broke up a real loaf of bread and gave a "sermon" that sounded like a wise friend sharing some kind words. I could imagine Jesus hanging out with his disciples in the same way.

I meet with Father Carroll in a glassed-in area behind the nurses' station in 2-South. Although the door is shut and supposedly no one can hear, the surrounding windows make the room a hall of mirrors. I can see a nurse. And I see her ghost nurse reflection.

I'm sitting hunched in a plastic chair. Father Carroll leans in too close and touches my shoulder. At least I'm pretty sure it's Father Carroll. Or it might be his demon twin. His breath isn't so great, and he's got giant flakes of dandruff on the shoulders of his crumpled-up black priest suit. I've noticed before that when he speaks his voice sounds slushy, like there's a lot of saliva in his mouth. I used to think this made his voice friendlier, but today it sounds weird.

I decide to say some stuff anyway.

"I've been having a lot of dark thoughts."

By this I mean thoughts of suicide, but I don't tell him that. God hates suicide. The nuns always said that Judas went straight to Hell after he hanged himself.

I expect Father Carroll to ask what the dark thoughts are.

Instead he says, "God doesn't judge us for what we think. We can be held responsible only for the choices we make."

What? That's weird.

That is completely different from what I was taught in grade school religion class. The nuns said God was constantly poking around in our brains, on the lookout for bad thinking, especially "impure thoughts."

"What about God's punishments?" I ask. I'm thinking of a childhood prayer:

"I detest all my sins because of Thy just punishments."

"I think God is more interested in forgiveness than in punishment," Father Carroll says. "Sin is not that big of a deal."

Sin is not a big deal? A priest would never say that.

Father Carroll smiles and gives a little laugh.

Is he making fun of me?

"Sin just means we made a mistake. We missed the mark."

I remember hearing something like that in high school religion class, I think.

"God isn't standing there with a stick," he says.

That's another odd thing for a priest to say. I look up at his face. He still doesn't look entirely right. His face skin is too wrinkled, and he has a pasty glow. But I decide chances are best that he's the real Father Carroll.

"How about I pray for you?" he says.

"Okay."

He touches my shoulder again and says a nice, solid prayer for me.

After Father Carroll leaves, I decide he really didn't say anything that weird and that his non-serious attitude is best.

I write in my journal:

"God not standing there with a stick."

A gentler picture of God was not entirely foreign to me.

When I was about six years old, I was playing in a quiet, wooded glen at the far end of my grandmother's back yard. The sun shone down through the shadows of the trees. I was focused on playing with a pile of leaves, but I also sensed a benevolent presence looking down upon me from the trees, smiling, enjoying me and my play. I had no theological words then, but looking back, I would say it felt like a divine presence, a connection with a loving God.

By fifth grade, any such notions had been obliterated by religion class.

In high school, however, one religion teacher talked of a god of "unconditional love," who cares about you personally. Although my meeting with Father Carroll revives this possibility, I fear that if the punishing god is the One True God, He will be extra brutal to those sinners who deny Him in favor of the wimpy "god of love."

That evening, I see more images of starving children on TV. I insist that my mother bring my checkbook on her next visit. When she comes, I write out a $250 check to CARE and make her promise to mail it.

At our next session, I ask Dr. Hardaway again about the starving children. I ask him how God could allow such horrors. I ask him about his own religious beliefs.

Dr. Hardaway says I shouldn't personalize what I see on television. He also tells me it's time for electro-shock therapy.

In my delusions I see myself as the deserving victim of punishment, but this is real. A small clearing opens up in my mind. Nightmarish fantasies of being tormented by demons drop away, replaced by the reality of Marie in her rollaway bed. This man will happily put electrical nodes up against my temples and blast my brain.

I tell Dr. Hardaway we won't be doing any ECT.

I'm surprisingly confident as I phone my parents to insist that Dr. Hardaway be fired.

"All they do here is drugs and shock treatment. I need psycho-analysis," I tell my mother.

My dad talks with some colleagues in the psychology field and finds me a new doctor. His name is Dr. Leighter. My mom tells me that Dad says he's "a good couch man."

Daily Journal

Feb. 27, 1979

Played bowling. Tremendously
happy feeling of community.

Fr Caroll stopped by. Sin
and big deal. God not standing
there with a stick. At first
I was depressed but later figured
his non serious attitude is best

EIGHT
CHECK IT OUT

*Told Hardaway I didn't want to talk. Get new doctor
tomorrow. Hope it works out.*

—Journal entry, February 1979

Dr. Leighter and I meet in a room tucked away off the main corridor on
2-South. I sit on a short couch under a window. He sits in a large beige
leather chair. He has a black moustache like a character in a Western and
a slow Texas drawl. Like all the psychiatrists at the hospital, he wears a
three-piece suit, but unlike the others', Dr. Leighter's is powder blue.

Dr. Hardaway is the Bad Guy and I desperately need the Good
Guy to ride into town. I look at Dr. Leighter's face. It looks okay. He
looks steadily back at me.

I start talking about my visit home. I tell him how weirdly bright
the rug looked. I tell him about not being able to understand what
people were talking about sometimes.

He seems to be handling what I'm saying so far. He's responding
like a normal person.

I bring up the worries I had about Janet's Krazy Mixed-Up Salt.

"You could have checked that out," he says.

"What do you mean?"

"I mean ask someone about it. Since it was worrying you."

"Like who?"

"Well, who could you ask?"

I hope he doesn't do this "answer-a-question-with-a-question"
routine too much.

"Maybe my mother?"

"Sure."

"Ask her if there is LSD in the salt?"

Sounds pretty crazy to me. To ask that.

"When you start thinking something like that," he says, "you can check it out."

I ponder this. There's no way my mom could *prove* to me there was no LSD in the salt. She's not a chemist. Nonetheless, I see that it would be possible to get her opinion.

Nothing horrible has happened yet, so I'm considering telling Dr. Leighter my deepest secret. The stakes are high. If he's an imposter, and I reveal that I see through the charade, he will end the suspense phase of my punishment and begin my *real* torture in Hell. I have pictured this moment many times, just as in fifth grade I imagined again and again waking up after death to face a disgusted giant Jesus and the Final Judgment.

In either case, I end up strapped to rusting medieval equipment while sweating, howling demons perform on me every torture I've ever feared, from the roasting of Saint Lawrence, to the freezing of Nazi prisoners, to the slow extraction of my tongue and fingernails. And it goes on for all eternity.

I look again at Dr. Leighter.

I feel like when I jumped off the high dive for the first time. I looked down at my ten-year-old toes hanging over the edge of the board and understood that there was an instant when you had to either go or stay.

That time, things had worked out. The water engulfed me, held me in its thrilling rush around my body, and then I bobbed proudly to the surface, knowing Mom was watching.

This time I don't know what might happen.

I take a breath and blurt out, "I think I'm going to be tortured."

Dr. Leighter looks pretty much the same. He nods and asks me to say more.

I tell him I think that I might be dead and in Hell. I tell him about the time I thought my family was going to torture me in the garage with my father's tools.

For the first time, I hear the ideas that have been racing around in my head for a month form into sentences and come out of my mouth. I see Dr. Leighter quietly listening.

I ask him what he thinks.

He says in his slow drawl, "Well, I don't believe that people want to harm you."

As I walk back to my room, the hallway seems a bit wider, the corners and doorways free of lurking devils. Although I can feel the terror trying to revive itself, the engine doesn't catch.

But back in my room, the door handle is still too high.

Even before I landed in the nut ward, the universe had been getting shaky. Particularly during the summer of my breakup with Laurie, I found myself worrying about the spooky implications of modern physics: the theory of relativity, the Heisenberg Uncertainty Principle, and the odd behavior of unobserved subatomic particles. A space-traveling twin returned to Earth, young and healthy, to find his brother had become a broken old man. There's a cat in a box, alive until the moment you open the lid to check on its health. Perhaps Hell literally exists as an eternal descent into a black hole. Einstein screamed "God does not play dice with the universe!" and then gave proof that He does.

There was some promise of liberation in these ideas: the destruction of Newton's impersonal clockwork cosmos, a justification of poetry, and the possibility of finding God. Perhaps a cosmic God is swimming amongst the tiniest particles or maybe He's bodysurfing on the itty-bitty waves.

On the mental ward, these ruminations get even more complicated.

I'm chatting with Larry in one of the small side rooms on the ward. Larry's a nice guy. Suddenly, I see a purple Bic Clic pen on the windowsill. I feel a shock of recognition. I own a purple Bic Clic.

Is that my pen? Did I leave it there?

I touch my pockets. No pen.

I'm always leaving stuff somewhere, but I don't think I've ever been in this room.

I stare at the pen.

What's holding it together? What's keeping it in that spot?

It's deteriorating slowly, shedding electrons. Furthermore, the atoms in that pen could fly apart at any moment. That's the Uncertainty. Maybe this is a quantum physics universe, where particles move from one place to another without passing through the intervening space. I've already closely observed the illogical behavior of water droplets. If there is a swath of light beaming into the shower, the droplets seem to get swept up in it and bounce differently. I've also carefully studied dust motes floating in planes of light.

I wonder if Larry can tell I'm freaking out.

"Is this my pen?"

I point at the pen. He sees it. His left eye twitches and his hand jerks forward awkwardly toward the pen.

"Is it?" he asks.

I leave the pen and Larry before things get any weirder.

I walk into my room and, in a panic, see that my purple Bic Clic is right there on my hospital table. I sit on my bed and stare at it. It looks *exactly* the same as the one I saw when I was with Larry.

Its molecules could have flown over there and then flown back. Why don't we ever see this happen? Observation changes the experiment! That's why the cat is still alive as long as you don't open the box.

Laurie had a studio apartment that was one big white square room. One day we were lying on the bed and she pointed out the crown molding that ran all the way around the ceiling. She said the ceiling was a lid.

"While we sleep, our giant keeper opens the box from time to time to check on us," she said. I laughed.

She was so smart, so funny, and I blew it. I screwed up. I lost faith in our love. I succumbed to my Uncertainty. There will never be another girl like her.

My purple pen stays put as long as I keep watch.

Twice I've been busted down to zero, strapped into my bed in a locked room. Now allowed only to wander around the secure ward, I dream of those glorious days less than a week ago when I could roam anywhere in the hospital, take a walk outside, sign myself out for passes.

Over several sessions, I ask Dr. Leighter the questions Dr. Hardaway ignored. Why are the elevator doors different? Why is the security room ceiling so high? Why are there metal strips along the walls? Why are there weird pipes and fittings everywhere? Why are the door handles so high?

Probably the elevators had different manufacturers or were installed at different times, he says. That's why one of them has two doors and the other has three.

Okay. I guess. But it's still weird.

Maybe the dark walls in the security room make the ceiling look higher, he says.

Later that day I investigate. I check the ceiling in Room 262, then quickly move to the next room, a regular one. I look up and... you know... they do look like they are the same height.

I checked it out.

Score one for Dr. Leighter.

The metal strips on the hallway walls are to protect the walls from gurneys that are wheeled through, he says.

Yes! That makes perfect sense. This is a hospital! I'll hold on to that one.

"The pipes and fittings are for stuff they don't use anymore," he says.

"But there are so many of them."

"It's an old building."

"But where do they go? What did they do?"

"I don't know. I don't lose any sleep over it," he says. "Sometimes you just have to accept things as they are."

The door-handle question doesn't go well.

"I think they do make the door handles higher in commercial buildings," says Dr. Leighter.

"Why would they do that?"

He doesn't answer.

The thought-accelerator in my mind revs up.

Hey, wait. People aren't any taller at home than they are in commercial buildings. This does NOT make sense.

I envision rows of arms with hands connected on the ends slowly reaching out toward door handles.

Dr. Leighter gets up out of his chair. He floats over to the door. He's like an awkward ghost. His gait looks as if his left hip is dislocated. His pale beige pants don't fall right. They're too clustered on his hip and the cuff around the back of his shoe is too creased. He puts his hand on the door handle.

"Yes, I think it is higher," he says.

Oh, shit, he's checking it out. He's got to check it out?

Dr. Leighter turns and looks at me. There's something wrong with his face.

I want to try reading again. I've always liked the spy genre, but I've never read a James Bond book. I remember I saw a copy of *Thunderball* at my aunt's house and ask my mom to bring it to me. I start in and find that, to my relief, I can follow the story. I'm making progress.

But within a few pages, Bond is being checked into a sanitarium. This seems impossible. I'm in a sanitarium. As the story continues, the details mirror my own awful life. Bond's nurse, Patricia, even has the same name as my nurse.

Dr. Leighter tells me you can find elements in any book that apply to your life. There are only so many stories possible.

Okay.

I guess.

But still.

It's weird.

I have to abandon Bond to his enemies.

I'm watching an old black and white movie from the 1940s on TV, alone in the day room. It's a Humphrey Bogart movie. I like Humphrey Bogart. He's tough, but he's a good guy.

But now Bogart has some guy tied in a chair and is pistol-whipping him. It's too horrible. I have to switch it off.

I tell Dr. Leighter I can't even handle an old movie on TV.

I imagine Dr. Hardaway would say, "What does that have to do with you?"

Dr. Leighter listens and says, "You have to deal with violence in the world the same way any of the rest of us deal with it."

But he doesn't tell me how the rest of you deal with it.

I mention to Patricia the trouble I'm still having with door-handle heights and elevator doors.

Her advice: "Don't focus on it."

Hmmm.

The weird stuff I bring up doesn't seem to bother Dr. Leighter or Patricia. Maybe I don't have to be bothered either.

The bedrock of Dr. Leighter's therapy seems to be this oft-repeated statement: "I like you, Joe, and I believe you are going to get better."

When feel afraid, check it out and see if it's really a threat.

—Journal entry, 1979

I've been free from freaking out long enough to earn Unaccompanied Grounds privileges again. I can go down to the cafeteria anytime and get a hot fudge sundae. It's that soft vanilla ice cream extruded into a yellow bowl and drenched in hot fudge. Delicious. I like the feel of the edge of the plastic spoon on my tongue when I lick the fudge off it.

I'm on a walk around the block in the early evening. I've been hearing radio news reports about a guy loose in this neighborhood, attacking people. At one point, he knocked on a door somewhere around here and stabbed the man who answered.

It could have been one of those homes across the street. I pick a house—a run-down one—and stare at its brown door. I imagine a man knocking. Another man opens the door. A knife flashes. The man stabs him. Blood. Screams. Terrible.

It bothers me that every night I go to sleep and I don't know what's going on. People sleepwalk. People black out and do terrible things and don't know what they've done.

It's getting dark. The killer is on the loose. I stop under a streetlight. I look down at my pants. I see a streak of brownish gunk on my pant leg below the knee. It's on my cuff, too. That's probably chocolate sauce from a hot fudge sundae. I must have spilled some.

But blood also dries brown. It's the iron. Oxidation.

How can you prove that you didn't do some terrible thing while you were asleep?

Check it out.

I walk up to the security guard at the hospital parking garage. He's always sitting in his little booth. The light is yellowish. The shadows are disturbed. The light flowing down on us is broken into little particles.

"See this on my pants?" I ask the guard. His forehead shadow falls abruptly over his eye sockets.

"Yeah."

"Does that look like blood to you?"

He looks.

"I think it's chocolate sauce," I say to him. "But it might be blood."

"Looks like chocolate sauce to me," he says.

"Okay, thanks a lot."

I feel better. I'm glad I checked it out.

NINE
MY FLUORESCENT GOD

Since I live in a nest of spies, the security guard has told Dr. Leighter about our little talk. Dr. Leighter wonders if I can still handle Unaccompanied Grounds privileges. I admit it was unlikely that there was blood on my pants. I admit I have no history of assaulting people.

I explain my theory about sleeping and blackouts and uncertainty.

"Do you think you hurt anyone?" he asks.

"No, not really," I say sheepishly. "But how can I prove it?"

"If you have more thoughts like that, talk to me about it, not anyone else."

Geez, I was just checking it out.

Despite the scolding from Dr. Leighter, I feel better. The next time I go to sign out, I half expect to find he's revoked my Unaccompanied Grounds privileges, but they remain intact.

From time to time, Dr. Leighter suggests I go back to 2-North. He thinks I would benefit from group therapy and the more intensive program. But I'm not going back to Roger and Grace's mind games. No way.

I have a new roommate. He's a bewildered old man. He doesn't seem to mind standing around wearing nothing but a hospital gown that he ties up the back, sort of. He has white wispy hair that twirls up off his head. He stands around staring much of the time, then shuffles his way around in a slow circle. He's like stop-action animation. I leave the room and he's standing at a certain angle, looking off. I come back ten minutes later, and he's in the same position but at a different point. Click. I come back again. Click. He's shifted.

Being the veteran patient, I have the window bed. He sleeps on the door side of the room. I worry about him at night. He sucks on butterscotch candies. I hear them rattling against his teeth. I hear him breathing around the candy. I keep thinking he will suck one into his lungs and choke.

I can't sleep worrying about him.

The nurse I think of as "The Annoyed Nurse" is in my room, straightening up. I tell her about the old man's choking danger. She says it's not my problem, it's theirs.

They never do anything about it.

One night, about 2:00 a.m., I wander up to the nurses' station and ask Sal, the matronly night nurse, for a sleeping pill.

"You've already got enough medications going," she says.

I have a like-hate relationship with the meds. I hate the side effects, but I like that they sometimes bring oblivion.

"Come on," I say. "Give me something."

"This might help," she says with a smile.

She hands me a lemon drop. I've always liked lemon drops.

"Thanks for the sleeping pill," I say. I smile back at her and plop it in my mouth.

"Anytime," she says.

From time to time, when insomnia strikes, I walk down the hall and get a lemon sleeping pill from Sal and we share the joke again.

> *Patient slept till 1 a.m. Then Patient got up and requested PRN lemon drop. Patient appearing cheerful and smiling, states no problem sleeping. Returned to his bed and slept remainder of night.*
>
> —Nurse's note, March 1979

I guess I'm doing a little better. Dr. Leighter has taken me off the hard stuff, liquid Haldol, and is giving me a pill called Navane. I hope some of my side effects go away.

In early March, Patricia and I discuss religion. I compare myself to several of Jesus' disciples. I say that sometimes I think I am "young and naïve" like John; other times like Thomas and "filled with doubts."

Part of my religious terror is God's mind game of faith. If you believe and show faith, you will be saved. But if you doubt, you sink and Jesus gets pissed off, like when Peter stepped out of the boat, got a few steps, and sank.

How can you *make* yourself believe?

Talking about this stuff with Patricia seems to help.

During a long conversation with Larry, he hits me with this:

"You seem to think that when something goes right it's luck. But when something goes wrong, it's your fault."

Father Carroll stops by again. We meet in the day room. Nobody else is around. I figure he's been talking with my mother, and I feel guilty and ashamed for causing her so much pain by still being hospitalized.

I tell him I hate being in here.

Father Carroll says that one of the reasons he likes Christianity is that it can follow you into a mental ward, or a cancer ward, or a death camp. By dying on the cross, Jesus led the way.

I tell him I'm afraid all the time.

He brings up that gospel passage he used at the funeral of my friend's dad. "Let not your hearts be troubled or afraid." He also says that throughout the Bible, God is always telling us to not be afraid.

I tell Father Carroll I feel hopeless.

"Jesus felt the same way," he says. "On the cross, even he felt that God had forsaken him."

Father Carroll says that God is always shining his love in our direction, even if sometimes we can't feel it.

"The story we know as the Prodigal Son is really more about the Father," he says. "Jesus paints a picture of who God is, a God of unconditional love. The Father goes out to check every day, hoping his son is coming back. When the son finally appears, there's no punishment, just a big hug and a welcome home party."

"But what about Hell?" I ask.

"Look, if anyone's in Hell, they would have had to work really hard to get in," says Father Carroll. "You would have to make a whole series of deliberate choices over and over again, because God is always offering forgiveness and love."

"But what about those passages in the Bible about weeping and gnashing of teeth?" I ask.

I'm not sure why I'm still arguing when he's telling me what I want to hear.

I call my mom and ask her to bring me the Bible that was assigned for my theology classes in college. It's the post-Vatican II translation called *The Jerusalem Bible*. She brings it when she visits in the afternoon.

When she leaves I look up some of the verses about God's love and about not being afraid. I'm tempted to look up some of the scary passages, too, but decide that wouldn't be good for my mental health.

I'm home for a visit at my parents' house. It's a blustery March day. I've just had lunch: a peanut butter sandwich, potato chips, pickle on the side. Sliced apple for dessert.

Never any complaints about the cuisine at Mom and Dad's house. Besides always having those lunch staples on hand, my mom makes terrific meat loaf, macaroni and cheese, tuna on toast, Spam in brown sugar sauce, pot roast, and Texas Hash, a combination of hamburger, onions, rice, and canned stewed tomatoes that was the first dish she ever cooked for my dad.

I'm sitting at the round table just off the kitchen, finishing up the apple, when my father breaks in on my comfort. He tells me he wants to talk to me, outside.

We step out onto the patio, which doubles as our basketball court, with a hoop mounted on the side of the garage. Growing up, I would shoot for hours out here, alone or with my older brother, late into the evening, even when it was rainy and dark, my hands slimy cold and cracked red numb. I wasn't sure it was still fun, but I didn't want to stop.

I see the giant weeping willow tree just east of the garage. My mother got nervous when my dad got up on ladders, but he fell only one time, when working on that tree. He hurt his back. It was bad, but not too bad.

Dad didn't go to the hospital. Never been. He wasn't even born there.

My father puts his arm around my shoulder, something he never does. He starts speaking to me, almost in my ear, like a coach or advisor, another thing he never does. He starts walking me around the patio, in a clockwise circle.

"Who's in charge?" he asks me.

"What?"

"Who's in charge?"

"I don't know."

He pulls me a bit closer. I can feel the strength of his body. I am 23 years old and he is 53, but he feels stronger than me.

"You're in charge," he says.

My father was born with a missing chest muscle, his left pectoral. He never talked about it, but my mom said he overcame this handicap with hard work. In PE he did all the exercises the other boys did, including climbing a rope. In 1942, at age 17, when he tried to join the Navy in World War II, he could perform all the physical requirements, but was turned down because the doctors saw his missing muscle. He joined the Merchant Marine instead and saw action dodging kamikazes on transport ships in the Pacific.

"Who's in charge?" Dad asks. "Say it."

"Me?"

"That's right."

I was also born with a bodily defect. There is something amiss in my lymph system. As a result, my right ankle is always thick, and my left foot is always a bit swollen. Unfortunately, my deficiency could not be overcome by an indefatigable spirit.

Throughout my elementary school years, I got a leg infection about once a year, condemning me to miss school for a week or two each time, moored on the couch in the living room, with the rest of family life buzzing about me. I felt ignored by everyone except my mother, my only lifeline.

I have a recurring desire for a dad who looks and sounds just like my dad, but this dad kneels down beside my sick-couch, claps me on the shoulder, and says, "Hey, champ! How are you doing today?"

But now my father does have his arm around me.

"Who's in charge?" he asks, one more time.

"I'm in charge?"

"That's right. Say it again."

"I'm in charge."

"That's right. Good."

I seem to have completed the assignment. He squeezes my shoulder and pats me on the back, something he never does. He walks me back into the warmth of the house.

The whole thing is awfully weird, but it somehow helps.

The next time I meet with Dr. Leighter, I wonder if he put my dad up to the "You're in charge" pep talk. But I decide not to mention it.

I do tell Dr. Leighter about something that is really bothering me. While Laurie and I were in the throes of our off-and-on breakup, she told me that my friend Fred had put a creepy move on her. I was shocked by her allegation. Fred and I had been best friends for years. Once, when I freaked out after eating marijuana brownies, Fred babysat me until I came down. Unlike a lot of guys our age, he was solid.

I had never known either Laurie or Fred to be a liar. My circuits were blowing. I wondered if this was a ploy by Laurie to lure me back.

Then, a month later, I mentioned Laurie's accusation against Fred to my first girlfriend, Theresa, who I was still friends with.

"He did the same thing to me shortly after you and I broke up," she said.

Now two women were telling me I had brought a creep into their lives. Worse still, in Laurie's case, I hadn't even believed her.

"Why don't you meet with Fred and talk things out?" Dr. Leighter says.

"I couldn't do that," I say.

"You need to confront some of the things that are bothering you," he says.

I set up a meeting with Fred. I feel nervous, which worsens as he enters the small hospital meeting room. He shakes my trembling, limp hand with his firm one.

I tell him what Laurie and Theresa said. He says something vague about different people having different understandings of events. He's smiling just like his normal self. I know he's not being straight with me, but I'm glad I said something. I look down at the table. The conversation ends with a brief attempt at pleasantries.

Marie is feeling better, so she's leaving. I say goodbye to her in the hallway by the front desk. She assures me I'll be getting out soon.

A day or so later, Dr. Leighter says, "I'm taking you off the Navane. You don't need it anymore."

We are standing next to the nurses' station and he has my chart open on the desk. He's erasing a row of daily orders for my medication for the following week. He's erasing my Navane.

Navane is a gentle-looking blue and white pill with a gentle-sounding name. I believe I need it or I will freak out.

I need my Navane. I need my Naaaa-vane.

"Well, can't we just taper it off...?" I ask meekly.

Dr. Leighter says something about blood levels.

In an instant, the lighting turns harsh and the shadows deepen. Dr. Leighter looks up. He's shorter than me, and now he seems to shrivel. He has dark circles under his eyes and every flaw in his skin stands out starkly. I see the lips moving on Dr. Leighter's pockmarked face. He seems to be explaining something, but all I can follow is the pencil eraser moving up and down in his hand, making dirty smudges in my chart.

The next morning, I'm pacing back and forth in my room. My limbs are shaking. The energy building inside me is too much. It's like trying to keep from throwing up when you know you have to.

There's nowhere to rest, no one to trust. Larry comes into my room. I tell him I'm getting scared. I start to take short, quick breaths, the precursor to the terror bark. Larry moves a half step closer.

I punch him in the stomach. He doubles up around my fist, his white nurse's coat flapping around my arm. He backs away and puts his hands out to protect himself. Immediately, I wake up to the impossibility that I did this. I don't hit nurses in white coats.

I say, "I'm sorry. I'm sorry. I'm sorry."

My hyperventilation turns into the terror bark.

Larry calls in another male nurse and they take me to Room 262. They put me in bed and lock the restraint around my waist.

At one point [patient] grabbed nurse by wrist and stated:
"Where's God? Is he here?"

—Nurse's note, March 13, 1979

Strapped down in Room 262 for the third time, I want to pray. But God—whatever that is—can't be trusted either. My images of the divine are a chaotic grab bag: Angry Judge, Non-Existent Void, Vaguely Benevolent Force, Loving Presence.

I want this last choice to be true, and it is to this God I start to pray, begging for a return of my sanity, promising that I will be more responsible, especially with regard to sex. I am shaking and sweating, sometimes yelling out, sometimes doing my terror bark.

A nurse comes in.

"Am I crazy?" I ask her. "Do you think I'm crazy?"

She doesn't have an answer.

I grab her by the wrist.

"Where's God? Where's God?" I ask. "Is he here?"

She frees her wrist and pats my arm. She leaves.

I stare up at the fluorescent light. I can't believe I am here again. *I'll never get out.*

My hair is matted with sweat. I clutch the black wooden rosary hanging around my neck and pray and plead.

"I'm crazy, can't you see I'm crazy? Please help me."

I kick the top sheet and blanket to the floor. I'm flat on my back, wearing only my underwear.

The light seems to brighten and hum. The light particles, pale and multi-colored, float down in a slow cascade. They are like the tendrils of a translucent glowing jellyfish, falling and swirling around me. At the same time, I am aware that I am staring at a plastic light fixture. The room fills with a sense of presence. This is more than the abstract idea that God exists. It is more than an awareness of a benign omnipresence. I do perceive a presence, but it is also perceiving me. It sees *me*, recognizes who I am.

I seem to hear God speaking, not an auditory hallucination, but a spiritual communication.

"Hi, Joe. I'm here."

"Really?"

"Really. I'm really here."

Light floods my body, its molecules intermingling with my own. The spiritual message continues:

"It's okay. I'm here."

I float a bit off the mattress, enveloped in a luminous pulse, buoyant on a wave of eternity, even as I remain aware that I am lying flat on a sweaty mattress in a mental hospital, a restraint around my waist, staring at an overhead fluorescent light.

The next day Dr. Leighter and I discuss yesterday's freak-out. I tell him most of what happened, but I leave out the God part. That would sound too crazy.

TEN

TREADMILL

*I think what bummed me out was seeing the reality of my situation
more clearly as I got healthier, so I also got more depressed.*

—Letter to a friend, 1979

*Able to smile, sense of humor returning, but has come back to me
several times asking "I hope you'll still talk to me as you usually do."*

—Nurse's note, March 1979

Much sooner than I expect, I'm out of Room 262 and back in my regular
room, where my roommate is still shuffling around in his circle.

At that day's therapy session, I tell Dr. Leighter, "It's weird. I feel
pretty normal, like I did before I lost control. But I'm scared it will
happen again."

"Well, sometimes there are minor setbacks," Dr. Leighter says in
his slow drawl.

"Do you think I can still start physical therapy today?"

"I believe so. You're doing fine."

Being told I'm less crazy makes me feel less crazy, so with a bit of
confidence I make my way to the physical therapy department, which
is up several floors. I take the grand central staircase.

I'm determined not to act crazy. The physical therapist says her
name is Bonnie. She's pretty, with straight brown hair. She's energetic
but real, not like Mandy with her plastic cheerleading and Snickerdoodles.

We walk into an area filled with weights and exercise machines. There is one other patient here, a guy who is poised between two long wooden rails. He gives me a nod. He's learning to walk again. No crazy people here—just a couple of guys who want strong legs and ankles.

Bonnie has me do toe-ups and the stationary bicycle for the ankle sprain, then adds in sit-ups, push-ups, and arm curls. She doesn't treat me like a mental patient and I don't treat her like a mental health nurse. I feel more like my old self when we're done.

Back on the second floor, I walk through the ward's double doors, turn left and head for my room. As usual, I'm looking at Ray. Ray is 35 and always sits cross-legged at the end of hall, his back against the wall, under a big, metal-mesh reinforced window. He's there any time they'll let him. He rocks back and forth and mumbles and yells out once in a while. He's got wild scraggly hair and a beard.

But today something is different.

As if waking from a dream, I see a strange sight: a disheveled guy with scraggly hair down at the end of the hall, sitting cross-legged, rocking back and forth and mumbling, yelling. He looks like a caricature of a lunatic in an insane asylum.

Yes, Ray's the same, but something is different—within *me*. Ray is bizarre, wacko, and disturbing, but it's taken me this long to become disturbed. Don't we have someplace to put nut jobs like him? Oh, yeah—*this* is that place.

I go to my room and sit on my bed, looking out the window. Less than a mile away, my former workplace is humming along, someone else doing my job.

I look at the cabinet next to my bed. It's stuffed with things I asked Mom to bring me over the past six weeks: the science book, the history book, James Bond and the Purple Crayon. My cousin Joanna brought me a simple flute-like instrument. I took it out of its bag one time. And there is my crappy work from Occupational Therapy: the copper owl rubbing, macramé, an unfinished knitted pot holder.

It's a cabinet full of failures.

That evening, I have dinner in the cafeteria with my cousin. I tell her what a loser I am.

"Oh, Joseph," she says.

As I head back into the ward, my elderly roommate shuffles slowly out into the corridor in his hospital gown toward where Ray is still rocking. I step into our room and approach our shared sink. On the floor beneath it, I see a small pile of shit. I bend and look closer. I almost expect it to be brown plastic from the joke shop, but it's real, just like an animal would leave. Coiled pale brown turds.

That's enough detective work, but one question remains. What am I doing in here? These people shit on the floor. They park themselves at the end of the hall and rock and mumble to themselves. They let themselves be electro-shocked in the brain. They're strapped down screaming and rattle the bed rails.

My delusion of a post-death adventure, wrestling with ultimate darkness and the fate of my immortal soul is terrifying, but it has more meaning than this reality: My life has come to a halt at 23 years old, and all that's left for me is to finish out a pathetic, institutionalized existence.

Who would I rather interact with?

1) An overburdened nurse, annoyed and bored, giving me a patronizing smile?

or

2) A wily demon, disguised in a nurse's uniform, fixing me with a spine-chilling grin?

To the nurse I am one more warehoused loser. To the demon I am a special person, deserving special treatment.

There are no demons here. The doctors aren't devils. Just guys you can't trust. I never died and went to Hell. I'm alive in the same old life I ever was in—the life where you can't trust your best friend, the children are starving, the love of your life is gone, your friends have abandoned you, and you'll never be able to work again. This reality is too much to bear and I freak out again, trembling and yelling.

The next four days are a blurry mess. I'm not tracking all the meds I'm given, but the medical record shows that during the next week I am prescribed Haldol (an antipsychotic), Valium (a "minor" tranquilizer), Stelazine (anti-anxiety/ antipsychotic), Cogentin (side effects), Nortriptyline (antidepressant) and, as a last resort, Sodium Amytal (barbiturate).

Patient now sedated with Haldol. He is drowsy but able to converse. Not able to articulate clearly but can be understood without problems. He continues to fear possibility of not

*recovering. He now has had at least two episodes of loss of control
following improved states. This is usually precipitated or associated
with trips home and other social stress. There is no clear pattern and
no significant response to medications except for sedation.*

—Psychiatrist's note, March 1979

Sedation—or rather oblivion—is what I want. Subconsciously, I'm
pleading "Drug me up, doc." But, as is often the case when bingeing on
drugs, consequences and remorse come crashing in. My side effects get
worse, especially loss of muscle control.

One night, I get up onto my bed to go to sleep. I find I am frozen
face-up, jack-knifed into three sections, like a jagged Z. My heels are
dug into the mattress, my knees are stuck in the "up" position, and I
can't lower my back and head. I can move my arms, so I pull the covers
over me. An inner dialogue commences.

Brain: *All right. It's bedtime.*

Body: *I know that.*

Brain: *So lie down.*

Body: *I can't.*

Brain: *You're not paralyzed. You got up here. LIE DOWN!*

Body: *Don't yell at me. I'm trying. Something's not hooked up.*

Brain: *This is insane.*

Finally, I call up maximum energy:

One, two, three… Go!

Something clicks and my body folds down flat. I wake up eight
hours later, still glued flat on my back.

Dr. Leighter orders a brain-wave EEG test for me to see whether
my freak-outs are the result of small seizures. I go to a little room in an
obscure wing of the hospital where an unsmiling doctor wires up
electrodes to my head. He twiddles the knobs on his machine.

It turns out there is nothing wrong with my brain, at least not in
the electrical realm.

Joseph was quite sedated in early am. Appetite fair, color pale.
Some drooling, walks with a shuffle, very slow in all movements
and speech. Quite childlike in behavior with many questions...

—Nurse's note, March 1979

I'm eating breakfast in my room. Nurse Patricia comes in and sits in my visitor's chair and asks if I want to talk. I don't answer.

"Let's review your current treatment goals," she says. She puts a sheet of paper in front of me.

I read: "Push Fluids. Do More For Yourself. Express Needs More Directly."

Dr. Leighter and Patricia have been on this "assertiveness" kick for me. Along with "taking responsibility," I'm supposed to "speak up for yourself." I'm struggling again to get past the first few pages of *Your Perfect Right.*

Patricia starts hassling me about getting dressed.

I say nothing, but I don't see the point. I know the routine. Soon I'll be walking around the ward in my own clothes. Then I'll get Accompanied Grounds privileges, then Unaccompanied. All the while, people will say:

"Can't you see you're getting better?"

But the craziness will secretly build and the false ego membrane will puff up, getting thinner and thinner, and I'm faking it and faking it until I can't take the pressure anymore. Then I will have my next freak-out.

Why get back on that treadmill?

I am very afraid.

"Do you think I can handle the shower?" I ask Patricia.

"I'm sure you can," she says.

"I can't untie my gown top," I say. "Can you do it?"

She looks at me as if I'm a child. I notice I am drooling, and I wipe my mouth with my sleeve.

"I think you can do that yourself," she says, looking at the knot hanging down behind my neck. "It's tied very loosely."

I've fiddled with the knot and my fingers don't work so well, but I also know she's right and that I just want Mommy to take care of me.

"Okay, okay, I can do it," I say.

I decide not to shower that day.

In my journal I write in a shaky hand:

The squeaky wheel gets the grease
The loudest bird gets shot.
An empty barrel makes the most noise.

My old man roommate is gone, discharged, evidently because he is no longer crazy. I never saw any improvement.

The next day, I'm talking to Patricia in my room.

"One of the last things my girlfriend said to me was that she's going to marry that new guy. They're getting married this month."

I keep forgetting to call her my *ex*-girlfriend.

"Are you sad about that?" Patricia asks.

I remain quiet.

Patricia makes sympathetic sounds but doesn't say anything to help.

I tell her I feel like dying.

She asks me to say more, but I don't have anything else to say.

Soon she starts in again about me getting dressed.

"That's a bit too much pressure for me," I say.

She says if I got dressed I could go out on the ward and talk to people, or play a game.

My voice sounds shaky, but I speak up for myself.

"I appreciate you following through with me, but the doctor said I should make my own decisions."

I agree to work with her on straightening up my room. Despite my embarrassment, I see a bit of humor in the ridiculous amount of stuff I have collected and make a joke about it to Patricia. She smiles. I tell her I will send some things back with Mom on her next visit.

Then I'm suddenly afraid that Patricia's mad about me not getting dressed.

"I hope you'll still talk to me the way you usually do," I say.

She says she will.

Later that afternoon, after Patricia has left the hospital, I get dressed and go out to the day room and join a card game of Hearts. My playing is clumsy, but I have some fun. I look up and am surprised to see Marie approaching the table.

"I just needed to come back," she says.

It's nice to see her, but I'm bummed out that she couldn't keep it together out in the real world. She seems less upset about this than I am. She joins the game.

The next day Marie starts another round of shock treatments.

At that day's session, Dr. Leighter suggests we take a walk around the block. As we leave the building, the air feels cold and foreign.

"After I'm inside the hospital womb for a while, regular weather feels alien and weird," I say. "I'm always so paranoid."

"Anyone can be 'paranoid' the way you use the word," he tells me. "It's normal that the outside feels different after you've been inside so much. It's normal that you wonder what a nurse meant by something, or how someone feels about you. But the real paranoia, which you had before—the fear of torture, the idea that there is a plot to make your life miserable—you don't have that anymore."

"Yeah, I guess I don't have those super-paranoid thoughts anymore," I say. "Those were because of the travel medication."

"I agree," says Dr. Leighter. "The Atabrine caused them and there is no reason why they should return."

It's good to hear Dr. Leighter's optimistic view, but I still sometimes question reality, like when I see something strange in the newspaper. One day I read a story that claims there was a nuclear meltdown at a place called "Three Mile Island." This sounds like apocalyptic science fiction. What kind of name is that for an island? It's too mathematical.

In a few days, there's a front-page photo of President Carter visiting the Three Mile Island facility. Impossible! There's no way a president would set foot in a place that is radioactive. I stare and stare at the picture.

I show the paper to Dr. Leighter. He claims it's real. This forces me to either accept it, or decide that one of the few people I trust is in on the fake-newspaper conspiracy. I look at him suspiciously, but his face doesn't get weird.

I guess sometimes you just have to go along with unbelievable things.

I make it back to physical therapy. Bonnie gives me a pretty smile, I nod, and we get right to work. She puts me on the treadmill. At first, my legs feel stiff. But as my speed and breathing increase, I notice both a thrill and a fear rising. I imagine myself strong and sane, walking down the street a free man. I feel invigorated, but I also feel I could spin out of control. It's the same tense, hyped-up feeling I had when speaking up in group therapy back in 2-North.

Two thoughts fight it out in my mind:

This is great! I'm strong enough! I could make it out there!
No you can't! You're weak! Don't risk it!

The squeaky wheel gets the grease
The loudest bird gets shot
An empty barrel makes the most noise.

ELEVEN

ROMANTIC INTERLUDE

Dear Tut — Thank you for all the good times and good feelings you've given me. I don't think I've ever cared so much so fast for anyone before.

—Note to me from a fellow patient, March 1979

As usual, Sunday stretches on forever. I'm alone, sunk into a worn beige couch in the day room, squinting into a blast of harsh afternoon sun. Patricia, Dr. Leighter, and the physical and occupational therapists are all off duty today. The sun makes the dusty air visible and heavy.

The click of shoes approaches.

"Hi."

It's a new patient, a young woman close to my age. She wears blue jeans. Her straight, raven-colored hair brushes the shoulders of her blue-green floral blouse. She's tall and fine-featured.

"My name is Melissa." She sticks out her hand.

"Joe."

I shake her hand with my soft, medicated grip. She sits down at the other end of the couch and starts in on small talk: the staff, the food. She gives me a sparkly smile.

I've been taking a break from romance and sex. I'm not even masturbating. It feels like I've just lost interest, burned out on that area of life. But no doubt the meds, depression, and anxiety play a part, too.

Melissa continues to chat. I note that she has gorgeous almond-shaped eyes and that her upper chest and neck are marred by circular scars, like she had a bad case of chicken pox.

She smiles again and I wonder hazily if she might be flirting with me.

My first romantic feelings were not for a real girl but for Alice, of Wonderland, who flickered to life on my family's TV set in the mid-1960s. Alice, with turned-up nose and round cheeks, gazes at herself in the looking glass, about to step through. I gaze at Alice. Foreign feelings sneak in, like seawater seeping into dry marsh. She is so pretty and this soft, delicious yearning is so unexpected, so delightful, so beautifully sad. I long to step through the screen and join Alice. Her magic black and white world glows more alive than the dingy colors of my family's living room. Everything else slips away, and a warm glow snuggles at the base of my brain. This dreamy state continues until, snug in bed, I drift off into a vision of Alice and Joe cuddling, 2-gether, 4-ever.

Occupational Therapy is much improved with Melissa sitting beside me instead of my mom. Our assignment is to make tile trivets. As Melissa helps me scrape the grout, our hands touch briefly. I look over and our eyes meet.

Dr. Leighter and Patricia both ask me, in the space of one week, if I'd like to talk more about my past relationships with girls. I'm sure they are in cahoots. They know that my ruminations about Laurie have figured prominently in my freak-outs.

I believe they have my best interests at heart, but I feel like a failure in this area and don't have much to say. But I start thinking about it.

I felt my first jolt of sexual energy also while watching the family television. James Bond's *Goldfinger* was all the rage. My dad and his friend Tom went to see it, but Dad said I was too young to go. This injustice was remedied when my brother and I got to watch *The Man from U.N.C.L.E.*, the TV version of Bond. My spy hero, Napoleon Solo, also drove fast cars, had lots of cool gadgets, traveled all over the world, and romanced a bevy of gorgeous women.

One Friday night, I watched with admiration and envy as Napoleon lounged in a deck chair beside the pool. He was dressed in a gray suit, white shirt with narrow tie, and he spoke into his secret pen communicator in his smooth, suave voice. A beautiful dark-haired woman in a black bathing suit tried to distract him. She kissed his face and nibbled his ear. He kissed her back, with a grin. He tapped his index finger on the tip of her nose and winked, then turned back to his pen.

I started noticing girls in real life. The closest one to Alice was Veronica, the cute blonde all the boys agreed was the prettiest girl in sixth grade. She sat across the aisle from me, and I gazed at her in gooey adoration. Veronica's blue plaid uniform skirt swooshed around her smooth, pale legs as she moved elegantly through the halls.

We also all agreed that redheaded Sandy and sultry, dark-haired Linda were the closest thing in sixth grade to the sexy Bond girls. They kept their uniform skirts as short as the rules allowed and ran around the playfield, providing an occasional glimpse of underwear.

In high school, in the early seventies, I considered myself a loser with chicks. Although I dated and made out a few times, and even had a sort-of-girlfriend for a while, I felt like a dork compared to the guys who were "getting some."

One weekend a group of us went to a friend's family farm on Whidbey Island in Puget Sound for our own hippie festival. We set up in an old barn. Out came the guitars and the air soon hung with the unifying smell of pot. The whole place glowed with brotherly and sisterly love. We ran laughing in the fields, our long hair blowing in the wind.

I got that romantic Wonderland feeling while watching a girl lying forward atop a horse in the middle of a hay field. She wore a yellow peasant dress. The horse was barebacked and the girl was barefoot and her long blonde hair mingled with the horse's mane. But she was too lovely and I was too shy.

Later, I was sitting near the water and far down the beach it was James Bond meets Woodstock. One of my friends was skinny-dipping in the surf with two girls. I could just make out the sexy, naked bodies of the girls.

Finally, when I was 19, I got a real girlfriend. Theresa and I dated for three months and then we decided we were sick of being virgins. We snuck up to my third-floor bedroom in my parents' house. On our first try I leaned over her and my long hair fell into a candle and caught fire. She swatted out the flames. We laughed, and accomplished our mission. At last I had moved into the winner's circle.

But Theresa wouldn't join me in Wonderland. She kept jumping off of Cloud Nine. But when I tried to break up, I found I was hooked on having a girlfriend.

I discovered the "trapeze method" of relationships, lining up the next girl to catch me before letting go of the previous one. After several of these leaps and catches, Laurie appeared. I had found my Alice.

After four months of romantic intoxication, my relationship with Laurie gave way to the hangover of inevitable human conflict. It got worse as time dragged on. One day after yet another difficult morning at her place, she took my hands in hers. She looked up at me with her big blue eyes, pleading.

"I just want to devote my life to you."

Something gave way inside and I panicked, face to face with the threat of her devotion. I couldn't breathe, but I remained stone-faced. A week later, I told Laurie we should "take a break" and "maybe see other people."

In separating from Laurie, I sensed that Plan A—Alice—had failed. I reached for Plan B—Bond. If merging with one woman meant drowning in quicksand, perhaps I could stay afloat among a multitude of lovers. I decided to transform myself into an international swinger.

Conveniently, I worked for an English language school that attracted female students from all over the globe. I chased after international women, and American gals as well, usually running into a dead end. But I did manage to entangle myself with three women from three continents. Instead of the smug bliss I expected, I felt bad—whether I was winning or losing the game.

I felt guilty when a Japanese woman told me her friends had warned her about me. "They say you are playboy," she said. I didn't reply, but inside I was horrified. I couldn't deny the charge.

I felt humiliated when Nina, the Mexican girl I dated, told me that Hispanic guys are more passionate than Americans. Then I got involved with a clingy and hysterical California blonde who was awaiting sentencing for drug-smuggling charges.

As I tried to juggle multiple relationships with women as unstable as I was, I felt pulled in all directions. It was worse than the romantic quicksand. I tried Plan A again, begging Laurie to take me back. As I pleaded with her one hot afternoon in her apartment, I saw another man's brown suede jacket draped over a chair. She said she was engaged to marry the jacket's owner.

That summer, I felt like I was going crazy, but with the help of alcohol, a few buddies who would listen to my tales of heartache, and lots of intense journal writing, I more or less pulled myself together. But my psychotic reaction to the travel medication brought the wave of guilt and regret crashing in again.

I succumb to Dr. Leighter's and Patricia's invitation to talk about all this and dribble out bits and pieces of the story to each of them. Both listen patiently.

Melissa shows up at my doorway with her meal tray and we eat lunch together. She knows the nutritionist said I'm supposed to get extra calories so she insists I eat her dessert. She's not allowed to sign herself out for a walk around the block, so we stroll up and down the long ward corridor, sometimes arm in arm. She's almost as tall as me.

Melissa calls me "Tut," because I sometimes wear a black T-shirt with a gold-embossed head of King Tut, from a touring museum show I saw. Melissa is starting to make me feel like the boy king of the mental ward. I seem to be the only guy in here getting this kind of female attention. I develop a slight extra spring in my step.

We sit in the day room on the couch, talking and holding hands as the sun streams in.

Then one day, Melissa leans in and starts kissing me on the lips, stroking my back. I'm flattered by her advances and kiss her back passively, kind of like James Bond on heavy medication. When she gets up and walks away, I take a good look at her trim body, packed into nice-fitting jeans.

As making out now becomes our regular thing, I feel a tinge of libido emerge. I fantasize that it would be truly impressive if Joe the ladies' man returned to action here in the loony bin. Melissa and I both now have grounds privileges and I start to wonder what nooks and crannies of the hospital might host a tryst: a closet or maybe the shower room.

Jailhouse conversations supposedly start with: "What are you in for?" In the mental hospital, we ask that, too. Melissa and I have talked generally about how we each came to be here. She told me she was chronically "nervous" and that this is her third hospitalization.

I've noticed that what I thought were chicken pox scars on her neck and chest are unusually deep and maybe in a pattern.

During one of our couch make-out sessions, I ask her, "So... what are these scars?"

"Oh those," she says. "They're cigarette burns. But don't worry, I wasn't tortured or anything."

She shrugs and offers no further comment.

The next morning, I'm lying in a semi-conscious state when I notice Melissa is sitting on the side of my bed. She leans in and I come up jackknifed at the waist into her arms. I have the sensation of passing through some kind of science fiction time lag, iterations of myself popping up one after another in sequence—like a Cubist painting or the comic book hero Flash taking off at high speed. I reassemble into Melissa's arms. She's kissing my neck and lips, her black hair flowing around my face. She smells good. I hug her.

My hand touches the side of her neck and I feel her scars.

I don't know whether she even wants to let our kissy-face activities progress to sex, but I do know that my fantasy of two crazy people sneaking off to the shower room together is a bad idea.

I ease her away and say, "No, no."

We remain friends, but that's the end of our make-out sessions.

This is a turning point for me. In the past, I would have felt compelled to pursue a romantic dalliance with a pretty girl, whatever the circumstances.

Discharge time comes for Melissa. In the day room on the couch, we say our goodbyes. As a parting gift, I give her a blue tote bag that my cousin Joanna gave me. Melissa gives me a farewell note and a peck on the cheek. As I walk back to my room, I still have that extra spring in my step.

TWELVE
RETURN OF THE SNICKERDOODLES

A spell starts by building, building off the last spell. This time I'm goin' and I ain't comin' back. Bouncy. Jumping. Tension building up behind a wall.

—Journal entry, 1979

Physical therapy is invigorating, but it also makes me more frustrated at my tremors and stiffness, which are my fault because when I freak out so bad I get tons of drugs. At night, not sleeping, I thrash around with regret and self-blame.

The next night, I write in my journal:

"There's something in me that takes perverse joy in torturing me... The terror is so frightening."

I also write:

"Tonight I felt the strange feeling I can <u>choose</u> not to dwell on certain thoughts... It's not inevitable."

But the inevitable does seem to be closing in. I'm in my room talking with Patricia. I ask her to tell me the side effects of the medications. She says I need to ask the doctor about side effects.

"Why won't you talk about things?" I ask. "Why won't you talk to me like you always did?"

In a flash, the lighting in the room—and Patricia's face—change. Shadows become stark. I can see pockmarks in Patricia's face, big divots hewn out of her skin. It's happening again.

"You have dark circles under your eyes," I tell her.

"You're very observant," she says.

I sit up on my bed. I can feel the terror bark rising in me. Short and sharp. The sweat is starting.

"I think I need the posey."

"Are you sure?"

"Yes."

I don't want another trip to Room 262. I'm so sick of this.

Patricia gets the leather restraint and puts it around my waist and locks it in place.

"I think you can control this," she says.

They're always telling me I'm in charge and it's my responsibility.

But there is something different this time. The panic attack feels like a car engine trying to turn over. Rrrrr. Rrrrr. But it's sputtering a bit. It doesn't roar to life and take off.

I have a vision. The panic state opens up before me. I'm looking down a tunnel. It's rotating rapidly and made out of whirling brown twigs knitted into one another. I could slide down that tunnel and not come back this time. Let the whirling, sharp twigs take me away.

But there's also an inner whisper:

"You can go down there if you want to. But you don't have to go."

"Control yourself! Get it together! Sit up straight!" These are orders I could never follow. But the little voice has crept up and said:

"Let me show you something. What I show you is my gift to you."

And I am shown the tunnel and not-the-tunnel. Not-the-tunnel means I stay here in this room talking to Patricia, my friend Patricia, who works so hard for me. I stay in this room, this room in the hospital where I am an insane mental patient, where my father never visits, and which most of my friends avoid, but where Pete and my cousin Joanna visit and my mom comes almost every day.

I look at Patricia. Her face looks okay. I'm panting and sweating and I realize the barking has been happening a little, but the engine still hasn't fired up. It tries to catch a few more times and then dies out. I look down at the leather strap around my waist.

"Am I going to have to go back to Room 262?" I ask her.

"Not if you can control it. It looks to me like you can control it."

I take this to mean that she won't report this if I keep it together. We can keep this between Joe and Patricia and nobody else needs to be the wiser. I'm not going down the tunnel. Not this time.

Another nurse comes in with my dinner tray. I quickly pull the sheet over the posey so she can't see I'm strapped in. Patricia doesn't say anything as the nurse puts the tray on the rolling hospital table and leaves. Everything is cool.

I ask Patricia to unlock the posey. She does.

I tell her I'd prefer to eat with the other patients. She says go ahead. I pick up the tray and walk down the hall.

As I slowly gain faith in my ability to make small, quiet choices, Patricia shows up with "a tool to structure your day." She puts a sheet of paper on my hospital table, writes "Tentative Daily Schedule for Joe" across the top, and asks me to help her fill it in. Although I feel like I'm slogging through quicksand, I agree to wake up, dress, eat breakfast, and tidy my room by 8:30. Then the day stretches on with activities like piano practice, Occupational Therapy, and Community Meeting.

For four days, I obey Patricia's schedule, with her checking on me several times a day. When Patricia has a few days off, I take them off, too. Upon her return, I sheepishly admit my lapse. But my growing ability to stay within the structure of the schedule boosts my confidence.

I'm behaving so well that Dr. Leighter is now giving me Mellaril, a milder antipsychotic.

One day I climb all the way up the grand central staircase. I've never been up this high before, and I have no reason to be on the top floor. But I have Unaccompanied Grounds and can go wherever I want.

I look down through all the landings at the little rectangle of black marble on the first floor far below. I try to be subtle about this and not look like a mental patient. But I think:

What's wrong with these people? A short time ago they were worried about me being suicidal and strapping me down in bed and now here I am with the power to hurl myself over the edge, like I told them I wanted to.

But the sickening crunch at the end of the fall holds no appeal.

In Occupational Therapy we are once again gathered around our pale laminate table, awaiting instructions. With a beaming smile, Mandy makes an announcement.

"Today we're making Snickerdoodles!"

My stomach caves in. This is the same assignment we had when I first came to Occupational Therapy, dazed and stupefied, in early January. I quickly calculate that Mandy must cycle through her repertoire of activities every couple of months. By the time she gets around the wheel, she presents the first activity as brand new, figuring no one who saw it last time could possibly still be lingering.

This is where I came in.

I've got to get out of here.

Dr. Leighter must agree. He's relentlessly moving me toward discharge. He says I need to have more activities outside the hospital: visits with my cousin Joanna and my friend Pete, extended times at my parents' house.

He tells me to write down, step by step, the things I can do when I feel the anxiety coming on.

I write in my journal:

> *"If people seem weird*
> *Investigate scare*
> *Try to assure self before talking with others*
> *Lie down → calm yourself*
> *Exercise control"*

My mom takes me to visit a community mental health day treatment program and two halfway houses. Both appear to be dingy pits of chaos run by jerks. I choose the one across the street from a day treatment program, less than a mile from my parents' house.

I return to the hospital and Patricia compliments me on my success in finding a place to live.

Social Worker Snell comes to my room and reminds me that if the state is going to pay for the halfway house, I need to apply for welfare.

He helps me fill out the stack of paperwork I stashed long ago in my bureau drawer. I'm sure he's thinking that he's "enabling my dependency."

After I leave the hospital, where my insurance has been picking up the tab, I will be in "spend-down status." The $2,000 I have in my bank account, my entire net worth, will be sucked into the state's coffers to pay for my first few weeks of treatment. I've been cheap and fearful about money my entire life. My family history is one of struggling immigrant grandparents and parents raised during the Depression, but somehow I don't much care that my life savings will vanish.

Breakfast is often the only meal I eat on the ward these days. I'm in the hospital cafeteria meeting someone for lunch, or at my parents' house for dinner, and I'm having more visitors. I'm starting to feel a bit like the mover and shaker I used to be. The hospital has become a comfortable home base, and the only times I feel shaky are when I'm out on pass.

Sometimes when I return, I see Marie, often looking dazed, recovering from another round of shock treatments. We're friendly, but I feel a growing distance. I feel slightly superior but also guilty, as if I am abandoning her.

The further I get from my last dose of Haldol, the more control I have over my muscles. I want to challenge that macho nurse Terry to a Ping-Pong rematch, but it's hard to find the time.

Dr. Leighter has given me an all-day pass to my parents' house for Sunday. This will be the longest I've been away from the hospital since the night I stole my brother's car and tried to drive to Oregon. I'll arrive before lunch, then watch a Sonics game in the afternoon. The hometown NBA team is kicking butt this year. Mom and Dad and a couple of my brothers will be there.

The Annoyed Nurse is at the desk. She assigns me the usual curfew: 8:00 p.m. But—I suppose because I'm doing so well—she adds a twist: I can get an extension if I call in. I tell my parents this when they pick me up.

The Sonics win and the meal is great: Mom's Sunday pot roast with potatoes, onions, carrots, and gravy. At 7:30 we're sitting around the living room. I start thinking about the 8:00 p.m. curfew and the extension. My mind revs up.

If I can just call in and change the curfew, what kind of curfew is that? Think logically.

It's not much of a rule if the person it applies to has the power to change it.

I don't really need to be back at a certain time, but isn't being back at a certain time the definition of the word "curfew"?

If there's no curfew, it's like I'm already discharged.

Dr. Leighter has been talking about discharge a lot.

I feel queasy. I ask my mom if she thinks I should extend my time.

"I don't know," she says.

"I mean we're having fun, aren't we?"

"Yes," she says.

"Maybe we could play a game."

Everyone agrees we could play a game. But it seems like people are getting nervous.

What's wrong with them? Is there something wrong with me?

I call the hospital. The Annoyed Nurse answers. I tell her I want an extension. "Fine," she says. "What time will you be back?"

"I don't know."

This is too weird. One of my keepers is asking me when I'll be back. The panic rises.

"What do you think?" I ask.

"You tell me."

I really bug her, I think.

"9:00 p.m."

"Sure."

Is this a trap?

My mind is racing, like I'm trying to calculate a formula without any numbers.

"No, make it 9:30," I say.

"9:30," she says. "See you then."

Her voice seems to have a knowing smirk.

What does she know that I don't?

I hang up the phone.

"Okay," somebody says. "What game shall we play?"

They're rubbing their hands together with phony enthusiasm. It seems like everyone's expecting me to decide. I can't decide. Finally, I say Monopoly.

We set up the game.

Am I acting weird? Why is everyone moving so awkward and slow?

I start to think logically again.

They all knew I could get an extension, but no one suggested it.

I had to bring it up.

No one seemed to welcome the idea.

My own mom didn't want me to get the extension. My own family doesn't want me around.

I suddenly realize I picked the wrong game. There are too many pieces. I can't keep the money straight. I should have picked a simple card game. Like Hearts or Crazy Eights. But what makes the eights crazy? I can't remember. I can't take it anymore.

"I have to go back to the hospital."

Everyone is embarrassed.

"But you just called in for an extension," my mom says.

Everyone is looking at me. My mom gets up. My dad silently gets his coat and car keys.

"Okay, let's go," he says.

On the ride back to the hospital my heart is pounding. The Cadillac is a lumbering box. My dad drives too slow, looking straight ahead. Even Mom looks slightly annoyed.

When we get close, I tell Dad to pull up next to a side entrance.

"Are you sure you'll find your way back okay?" my mom asks.

"Yeah, I'm sure."

After two months living here, I'm the Hunchback of Providence Hospital. I know every entrance, staircase, lobby, and breezeway. If there were flying buttresses I would swing from them. I push the heavy Cadillac door closed.

I go up the stairs and head toward the big doors that lead into 2-South. I walk up to the nurses' station. The Annoyed Nurse is still there.

"I thought you weren't coming back until later," she says.

"I got too nervous," I say. "I need extra meds."

"What's going on?" she says.

"I'm afraid I'm losing control."

She looks skeptical. She checks the chart.

"What do you want? You can have Mellaril or Haldol."

More rapid thinking:

I've only been on Mellaril for a week. Mellow-rill might not do it. Not like Hell-doll. Mellaril is a pill. Haldol is a stiff liquid shot, sloshing down the hatch.

"Well?" she says.

"I can't decide."

"If you don't decide, we'll decide for you."

Decide for me? Shit. What would they decide? They always go with the Hell-doll, don't they? Or maybe she'd go with the Mellow-rill and it won't stop my freak-out. I couldn't stand another trip to Room 262. Better go for the hard stuff.

"I'll—I'll take the Haldol."

As soon as the little paper cup leaves my lips and the drug passes down my throat, I know I blew it. I fucked up. Just when I was getting free of the stiffness and the clumsy fingers, I wimped out and got dosed again. And this time, I did it to myself.

Why am I such an idiot? Fuckfuckfuckfuckfuck.

As I slink off to my room and climb into bed, my head is consumed by one of my fear mantras:

I'll be crazy forever… I'll be crazy forever…

The next day I explain to Dr. Leighter my logic about the curfew that is not a curfew.

"You have to learn to control your thoughts," he says.

He looks at me steadily for a long moment.

"I once had a patient who was a very smart man," he says in his slow drawl. "He spent his time writing complex formulas on a chalkboard, all of which were accurate and all of which came out to equal H_2O."

I nod.

"I had to get him to stop doing that," he says.

This hits home. We sit there a moment.

"I'm afraid I'll always be crazy," I say.

He reminds me that on my first visit to my parents' house, I saw my family as imposters, as torturers. This visit, I got swept up in intense social anxiety and unease about my upcoming discharge, but my grasp of reality stayed basically solid. Even though I went into a panic state, it was my least severe to date.

...It was discovered that with firm and constant reassurance, the patient could control his behavior and... [he realized] that he was not going to remain psychotic forever.

—Dr. Leighter's discharge note, April 1979

My single dose of Haldol doesn't bring on the side effects I feared, and despite the aborted home visit, Dr. Leighter keeps me on my march toward discharge.

I guess if he's not worried about it, I won't worry about it either.

The day before discharge, Dr. Leighter and I have a final meeting at the hospital. I'll continue therapy with him, but in his private office downtown. We review my plan for coping with anxiety and the logistics of my discharge.

He assures me again that I've gotten much better but reminds me that the halfway house will be lots different than the hospital. Residents must take their meds and attend the treatment program across the street, but other than that I'll be on my own. There will be no more signing in and out. My meals won't be brought to my room on a tray. I'll have to do my own laundry. There will be a much smaller staff, and I will need to interact more with my peers.

"It's sink or swim time," he says. "If you can't make it there, I'm afraid your next stop is Western State."

This reality check scares me, but I trust Dr. Leighter is not being dramatic. I know my insurance has run out and I'm running out of options.

Western State Hospital is the nuthouse of horrors several miles out of town, where Frances Farmer was. In my mind, it looms dark on a hill, like the asylum where the Joker often ended up wearing a straitjacket in the Batman comics I read as a kid.

"I think I can make it in the halfway house," I say.

"I believe so, too," he says.

My bags are packed and I'm looking at my empty room. I've made my bed for the final time. I feel numb, but determined to hold it together.

The hospital has gone from being a jagged, unstable hell from which I tried to escape twice, to the only place in the world where I feel more or less normal most of the time. I pick up my two suitcases and walk down the hall like a zombie—not from heavy drugs—but from the heavy fear I'm holding at bay.

Tonite I beat the strange
feelings I can choose not
to dwell on certain thoughts
Self-indulgent. It's not in-
curable

PART II
HALFWAY HOME

THIRTEEN

ROOM IN THE INN

*Phone call from Dr. Leighter. Joe must build from small
successes to regain his self-confidence. Joe needs a less-structured
environment right now.*

—My mother's journal, quoting Dr. Leighter, April 1979

*…I learn something new everyday, even if it's that Joanna
thinks you should put a burned finger into flour. Don't let
things get strange for you. Don't think about disappearing
pens. Just accept things.*

—My journal, April 1979

Leaving the hospital behind, hopefully forever, feels a lot different
than my visits out on passes. As the Cadillac rolls along, my anxiety
builds and my energy drains with each block my mom and I travel. My
brain is spinning with worries.

I can't cut it in the real world.

The Cadillac pulls up in front of the halfway house, which is called
"The Inn."

A phrase from the Bible starts looping in my mind:

"There is no room in the Inn."

And mine isn't ready yet. The director, who is scheduled to do my
intake, is at lunch. Mom and I drop off my suitcases in the office and go
across the street to the Seattle Mental Health Institute (SMHI), where I

will attend "day treatment." SMHI is on a small campus that takes up half a city block, with meandering walkways and low-slung buildings.

In the main office we find a social worker named Jane. She's small and lively with a halo of curly blonde hair and an ironic smile.

"Hello, Joe. Hello, Mrs. Guppy," she says, shaking our hands briskly. Jane gives us a tour of the facility, including the group rooms, the offices, and the library.

"We have basketball and volleyball in the gym," she says. She opens a big door, revealing a wooden floor court.

I always loved playing basketball, but I was never that good. I spent hours playing every day after school. Maybe basketball could get me going again. But I'm not sure I have the energy.

We go back to the Inn and my mom drops me off with Steven, the director, and says her goodbyes.

One end of Steven's office is rounded, extending up into a turret that protrudes from the roof. The architecture, leaded glass windows, and painted-over woodwork add up to a turn-of-the-century mansion gone to seed. I pick up my suitcases and Steven leads me through the shadowy front hall. I flinch when I see some of my new housemates shuffling around like undead ghouls. They are more unkempt than the chronics of 2-South. One old man with sunken cheeks stares blankly at me, then mutters something.

I slip back into the twilight zone feeling. Things start to seem frightening and unreal.

Steven pauses to introduce me to the one other staff member on duty. There is no cadre of white-uniformed psychiatric nurses to monitor our every move. Two blue-jeaned staff members oversee 40 residents, in various states of craziness and dishevelment, who come and go as they please.

We pass through the living room, where more housemates stare at a droning television. It would be impossible to discern the original color of the carpet. The furniture is dirty, beige, vinyl.

We push through a heavy fire door, walk up a long brown linoleum ramp that has a distinctive musty smell, take several right turns, and then Steven is knocking on a door. My new roommate opens it.

Ronnie has a mass of tangled black hair and torn jeans splattered with paint. He looks about 18 years old. Steven introduces us.

"Hello, Joe. Nice to meet you," he says. "Hee hee hee."

He has a slight Native American accent. His voice comes from deep in his chest but then takes a roller-coaster ride up and down the register. His giggles erupt into cartoonish mad cackles.

The room is a mess, clothes littered all over the floor. A transistor radio squawks in the corner. On his way out, Steven tells Ronnie it will be good for him to have a roommate again.

"Well, I guess that's your half of the room," Ronnie says, with a sweeping gesture. "Hee hee hee hee."

He speaks with a quick forward burst of energy but then draws himself back as if he's a court jester about to be struck by the king.

Ronnie starts kicking his stuff out of my half of the room. There are two green plastic-coated mattresses on the floor, angled crazily. I take one and pull it to the side of the room and arrange it against one wall. A water stain crawls down the cracking, pale yellow wallpaper. I put my suitcase on top of the bed and sit down on it.

That night, as I'm trying to sleep, I find out Ronnie is a babbler. He lies on his mattress and blurts out random stuff.

"I just want to get this over with."

Pause.

"No, no, no, I don't have to do that."

Pause.

"It smells good, it smells like shit."

Pause.

"Hee hee hee."

That afternoon, I take the bus downtown for my first therapy session with Dr. Leighter outside the hospital. We meet in his small, subterranean office. I look around and see a tiny window awkwardly crammed high up into the wall, with a Venetian blind that hangs down at an odd angle. I remember I'm not supposed to obsess about strange details.

Patricia says, "Don't focus on it." Dr. Leighter says, "I don't lose any sleep over it." I stop looking at the weird window.

I tell Dr. Leighter my roommate is freaking me out. He reminds me that learning to interact with my peers is one of the main reasons I'm there.

"Get to know him," he says.

Two days ago Ronnie kept me up all night babbling… he was just a dark shape looming out of the night.

—Journal entry, April 1979

The next day, I'm in our room looking out the window. It's a bright spring day. I see Ronnie on the sidewalk below. He's facing the Seattle Mental Health campus across the street. Suddenly, without looking left or right, he takes off and ends up on the opposite sidewalk. He pauses there a moment, then abruptly turns right, marches ahead about a quarter block, and briefly pauses again. Then he does an about-face and heads back toward where he started.

This random, stop-and-start walk continues for some time.

Ronnie isn't the only nut job at the Inn. There's me, for example.

I'm walking through the TV room. A bunch of housemates are vegged out on the vinyl couches. Only one of them laughs at the show they're watching, but his constant guffaws more than make up for the others' stony silence. It's a Tom and Jerry cartoon.

I've always hated Tom and Jerry.

Jerry the mouse wields a giant hammer and smashes Tom the cat on the thumb. The thumb swells to an impossible size. I slip deep into my twilight zone state.

Tom and Jerry are chattering at each other like denizens of Hell. The mouse has a satanic grin. I realize this message about pain and hammers is aimed right at me—referencing the time I thought I was going to be tortured with tools in my father's garage. This cartoon character is deliberately taunting me. I look around suspiciously. The couch zombies just stare at the screen.

I get out of there. But I can't stop myself from walking back in from time to time to see if the TV still has a special message just for me. It usually does.

That afternoon, I head over to my cousin Joanna's house for lunch. We're talking in her kitchen. I feel fairly relaxed around her. She's accepting in a low-key way. She asks me how I like life at the Inn.

"I've always wanted to live in a flophouse," I say.

"Oh, Joseph."

It occurs to me that maybe we get along so well because she's crazy, too. I try to remind myself that seeing other people as insane is part of my problem, like thinking my parents were going to be committed when they checked me into the hospital.

Joanna is heating a saucepan of her homemade pasta sauce. She burns her finger on the side of the pan. "Ouch!" she cries out. She rushes to the flour canister, pulls off its lid, and plunges her finger into it.

What in the hell is she doing? That's insane.

She pulls out the finger. For a brief moment, it looks like the tip of her finger is missing, but it's just covered in flour.

Uh oh. The weirdness comes on strong again.

I must have muttered something because Joanna says, "What?"

"What are you doing?" I ask. I'm checking it out.

"You always put a burned finger in flour," she says, annoyed.

"I never heard of that," I say. I hear the panic in my voice.

She looks crossly at me. She doesn't look like herself. I don't talk much for the rest of the visit.

When I get back to the Inn, I call my mom and tell her what Joanna did. She agrees that Joanna sometimes has unorthodox ideas. We both conclude that you're supposed to run cold water on a burned finger.

Dr. Leighter has a different take on the flour finger incident.

"Joe, I believe you can control thoughts like this," he tells me.

I can't do it, I think.

"Just because an idea is new doesn't make it 'weird,'" he says. "We all learn something new every day."

"What if this kind of stuff keeps happening?"

"You're doing well," he says. "Sometimes this process requires a little faith."

My first day treatment activity at SMHI is "Process Group." About 15 of us sit in a circle on folding chairs in a room colorfully and haphazardly decorated with construction-paper art we'd made earlier in the day to express our feelings. Mine is a dark purple blob.

Our social worker arrives, a few minutes late, and takes the one empty chair. The patients on either side of him shift their chairs a foot or so away from him.

He introduces himself as Alvin. He's wearing a clean white crewneck T-shirt, fresh blue Levi's, and brown loafers. He has wavy black hair and a cleft chin like a male model, although his cynical smirk lends him a smarmy intelligence. He seems to know something we don't, and since we're all mental patients on welfare, this would be a reasonable claim.

He begins group with a loud silence, during which he looks around expectantly. No one speaks, or even makes eye contact.

"This is *your* group," Alvin says. "What do you want to work on today?"

No one is talking, and I'm sure not going to be the first to speak up. We fidget in silence.

"Well, I guess nobody has any problems. Is that it?"

More fidgeting and staring at the floor.

"Is that how it is, Ken?" Alvin says, directing his attention to a patient across the circle. Ken is tall and thin, folded up in his chair like a praying mantis. "No problems?"

"Not really," Ken says in a flat voice.

"Let's see. You don't have a job. You're living off the state. And wasn't it you I saw out there spaced-out half-naked standing on the parking strip?"

Ken clenches his body tighter and stares at the floor.

"What was that about?" Alvin asks.

"Nothing."

"You keep that up and you're going to end up back in the hospital."

I'm starting to see why nobody says anything.

That afternoon, I'm out walking around and I see Ken doing his thing. He's standing catatonic on the parking strip outside the Inn. Punk rock is popular, but on Ken the spiky hairstyle doesn't look like a rebellious statement. It looks like the hair of a crazy person.

Ken stands still and upright. He looks up toward the sky. Intently. He seems to see something. Something riveting.

A half hour later, I pass Ken again. He's in the same position, but now his white shirt is unbuttoned, peeled down off his shoulders and hanging around his waist, still tucked in. The sleeves dangle down his legs, the empty cuffs lie on the grass beside his feet like excess appendages. His chest barely moves with his thin breaths.

I pause beside him. He doesn't seem to notice. I move next to him for a moment and stare at him the way he stares at the sky. He doesn't budge.

I want to ask him:

"What are you seeing?"

"What do you know from in there?"

"How can you not care what people think?"

Part of me wishes I could do something similar, but I don't have the guts for it. I do care what people think. I can't act that nutty even when I feel that nutty. I go inside.

Twenty minutes later I come out to check on Ken, and now he's standing in just his graying, tighty-whitey underwear, the rest of his clothes strewn around his feet. His legs are like a crane's legs.

He is so committed to his madness.

I trudge back to the Inn and into the dingy basement dining room to face the lunch menu: runny macaroni and "cheese" with a side of boiled carrots.

The next day in group, Alvin points out that if Ken takes off any more clothes, he'll get arrested. Ken says don't worry, he won't do that.

Audrey is another one of my scary housemates. She hovers around the house like a ghost and wrings her red, raw hands. She favors long-flowing, light-colored hippie dresses. She's pretty, but the part of her face that emerges through her long brown hair is scrubbed way too rosy pink. She has a whispery voice. She talks a lot about germs.

The therapists and staff at the Inn and at SMHI all spout the same party line. This whole setup—the residence with a treatment center across the street—is a "therapeutic milieu." It's ongoing group therapy where we crazies are supposed to form relationships and work out our problems with each other and the staff. We're *practicing* to be normal so later we can go out and *be* normal with normal people.

This sounds like bullshit to me. The Inn is a dump and SMHI is staffed by underpaid rookie therapists. We mental cases don't pay taxes. Few of us vote. We're society's lowest priority. They're just keeping us out of the way, fed and housed, as cheaply as possible.

That night, Ronnie's babbling wakes me up as usual. But this time he gets out of bed and says, "I'm gonna smoke one of them cigarettes."

The pack of Lucky Strikes is mine, on a table in the middle of the room. I smoke about two a day and don't want to get hooked so I don't inhale. For some reason it doesn't bother me that my smoking is something extra for my mom to worry about.

Ronnie shakes a cigarette out of the pack, lights it, and squats in the purple shadows like a hunched goblin. The smoke hits my nostrils.

Ronnie says, "When I finish this cigarette, you are going to die."

Pause.

"Hee hee hee. HA HA HA HA."

The end of the cigarette glows as he takes a puff.

"I just want to get this over with," he says.

I lie there, as still as I can, trapped in a room with a certified nut who's talking about killing me. The lone overnight staff person is two floors down and a maze of corridors away.

I think about how I can defend myself. Ronnie's pretty scrawny, but I'm pretty scrawny, too. He just sits there, smoking. Then he goes back to bed.

A half hour later, he's lit up again, squatting in the same place.

"When I finish this cigarette, you are going to die."

Pause.

"Hee hee hee hee."

I make up a plan that if I survive the night, I'll get one of the metal utensil knives from the cafeteria and stash it under my mattress.

The next morning, I forget about the plan to get the knife. But fear of Ronnie has awakened some part of me that realizes I won't last long here if I stick with the idea that all my housemates are zombies or psychos.

I've noticed a guy named Nick, who often holds court in the front room in the evenings. Nick is eloquent, with sandy hair and excellent diction. I'm envious because I've heard him announce several times that he's "going out for drinks with friends," something I don't think I'll ever be able to do again.

I spot Nick sitting alone in the basement cafeteria. I put my breakfast tray down on the table. He welcomes me into a chair with a grand wave of his hand.

We have the "What are you in for?" conversation. He says he got depressed last summer and took an overdose of Quaaludes.

"I almost died and ended up at Fairfax," Nick says. "What hospital were you in?"

"Providence."

"Fairfax is a cut above the Seattle loony bins," he says. "But it's expensive. I expect them to install coin-operated drinking fountains."

I manage a chuckle.

"Do you know my roommate, Ronnie?"

"Oh yeah. He's been around awhile," Nick says. "He's really fucked-up."

This isn't helping, I think.

"He sniffs paint. That's why he's so psycho."

That explains the paint splotches on Ronnie's clothes. It also ratchets up my fear. I'm living with a brain-damaged lunatic. But I'm pleased I got up the nerve to chat with Nick.

Out of desperation more than courage, I take Dr. Leighter's advice and start a "What are you in for?" conversation with Ronnie. He tells me he started drinking at age 14 and went wild. His family hung in with him for a while, then kicked him out when he got into sniffing paint.

"I tried to spray paint my lungs," he says. "Hee hee hee."

I start to see that Ronnie isn't a psycho demon, he's a screwed-up kid. He also says he escaped once from Western State Hospital. I'm impressed.

He tells me not to pay attention to the weird stuff he says.

"I'm just talking to my voices."

He says he hears them right now, mumbling in the background, like people sitting around the dinner table. He even hears their silverware clanking. But at other times, the voices give him orders.

"The voices tell me to do stuff, like go over here, walk over there," he says.

"I've seen you walking around out there," I say. I point toward the window.

"Yeah. The voices say cross the street. Okay, now turn around. Stuff like that. One time I was out on a dock and the voices told me if I jumped in the lake a beautiful girl would want to be my girlfriend."

"Did you jump in?"

"Yeah. Hee hee hee."

Pause.

"I got wet. But I didn't get the girlfriend."

From then on, I realize that Ronnie's babbling is not aimed at me. So when he starts talking out in the middle of the night I say, "Shut up, Ronnie. Gimme a break!"

Pause.

"Oh. Okay. Hee hee hee," he says.

And he shuts up.

For a while.

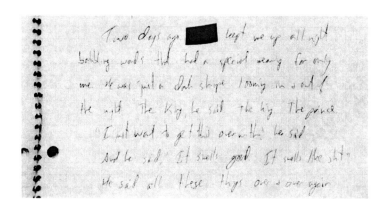

FOURTEEN

SMELL THE FLOWERS

The lethargy is upon me. "Goin' Down Slow," the title of an old blues song, starts looping in my head. Each morning I wake up, I have less and less energy. I resolve to get up by 7:00. One morning, I succeed and make it down the musty brown linoleum ramp to breakfast. Then I feel a seductive pull:

I want to go back to bed.

This thought is followed by a harsh rebuke.

Don't do it, loser!

As the inner argument rages on, I shuffle back upstairs. My bones feel like water and I lie down again on the bed, with my clothes still on. I pull up the covers and escape into unconsciousness, knowing I'll wake up to this inner monologue:

Weakling. Failure. You'll never get out of here…

The words of Jesus in the garden whine at me:

"Could you not stay awake a few hours…"

Lars is the other group leader. He alternates with Alvin. He's a tall, substantial fellow with a sparse brown beard and longish, light-textured hair.

Lars says the group topic is "feelings."

People start talking. Lars makes an occasional smart-aleck remark, but the patients speak freely. Like Alvin, Lars can be confrontational, but he does it with connection and humor. He also seems to genuinely appreciate our company.

I'm down on myself and numb today. I sit stiffly in my chair.

"I don't have any feelings," I say quietly.

"You have no feelings?" Lars asks.

"It's like I'm dead inside."

Lars holds me in his steady gaze.

"Suppose I said that you're a spineless twerp?" he asks, with distinct enunciation on the last two words. "Can you feel that?"

My face flushes and I feel a burn of anger in the center of my guts.

"Yeah, I guess I can."

I have to admit it. I also have to laugh at Lars' deadpan delivery.

As the weather warms, residents start hanging out on the Inn's massive, L-shaped front porch, which wraps around the front of the building. People talk, smoke, and space out. Occasionally, someone brings out the battered house guitar and sings. I can go out there and sit like one of the zombies if I want to, but if I want to pipe up and join in a conversation, I can do that, too.

As I become more comfortable with my housemates, I see that we can be divided into two categories. The patients I first saw as the walking dead are actually heavily medicated chronics, generally middle-aged or older. But there are also a dozen younger people like myself, Nick, and Audrey, who are "working on our issues," trying to make our way out of the system.

Bella is of medium build and wears black glasses like Elvis Costello. Her pale face is framed by dark curly hair. One evening, when several of us are sitting around the porch, Bella says, "Staff keep trying to get me to take a bath. But I'm depressed. I hate to take a bath when I'm depressed."

"How about a shower?" asks Nick.

"Same thing," says Bella.

"Your hair's clean," I say.

"Yeah, that's something I figured out a while ago."

"What?"

"Peggy was really bugging me to bathe. So I said okay, went into the bathroom, closed the door, and turned on the shower. Then I washed my hair in the sink. When I came out Peggy was all smiles."

We all sit there a moment.

"So now I keep my hair clean and she doesn't bug me."

I choose not to make any special effort to smell Bella, but she isn't reeking. Maybe she has naturally inoffensive body odor.

I like the porch because it's halfway between the halfway house and the full freedom of the sidewalk, where normal people walk. When I see them glance up at us, I wonder if they know what we are.

One day, Nick tells me there's a party with a talent show coming up at the end of the month.

"Just another lame attempt to get us to socialize," I say.

"Oh, come on," he says. "It'll be stupid and funny. There must be something you could do."

"Maybe juggling," I say.

The SMHI therapists are available for informal one-on-one counseling. I avoid Alvin but start talking to Lars. One day, we are walking along the winding sidewalks of the campus after group. He fiddles with his pipe, which he never seems to light.

"I am a complete fuck-up," I say, giving voice to one of my mental loops.

"Are you?"

"I used to be somebody. I got a good grade point in college."

"You sure are a fuck-up," he says.

"Whaddya mean?" I say.

"Well, you graduated, didn't you?"

"Yeah."

"You claim to be the world's biggest fuck-up, but you've already fucked up being a fuck-up. You shouldn't have got that bachelor's degree. You fucked up."

For a moment, my brain glitches as I take the circuitous trip through his logic. Then I laugh.

Lars got me again.

I get my juggling balls from my parents' house and start practicing. I'm thrilled to discover I'm far enough away from my last dose of Haldol that my old skills are back.

One early evening, some of us are hanging out on the porch. Nick again announces that he's "going out for drinks with friends."

I wish Nick would invite me out with him, but I know I couldn't handle it. A noisy bar, at night, with normal people who are strangers would make the weirdness come on strong. Even dinner at my parents' house still sometimes gets sketchy.

It's an empty Saturday. Nothing to do but wait for meals. Dinner is meat loaf again. It has a gray-green hue and the texture is boiled sponge. After dinner, TV.

There's a commotion as Nick barges in with Steven trailing behind him.

"What's up, Nick?" Steven asks, in an unnaturally calm voice.

Nick's face is bruised and his shirt is torn. One eye is blackened.

"I'm fine!" he yells, batting at Steven with his arms. "I'm just going to watch some TV."

Steven and another staff person move in front of Nick, blocking his way.

"Bullshit!" yells Steven. "What happened?"

"None of your fucking business!" Nick yells back.

I can't stand the yelling. I go to my room and lie on my bed with my clothes on and pull the covers over me. I look at the stains on the ceiling. Soon the yelling stops. I take a breath.

There's a tremendous crash. And then another. A girl starts screaming and doesn't stop. I want to go down and find out what's happening, but I'm scared.

The screaming turns to loud sobbing and I hear the clatter of feet, then sirens. I look out my window. An ambulance pulls up. Soon somebody is loaded into it on a stretcher. I'm pretty sure it's Nick. I get back into bed and lie there not sleeping for a long time.

The next morning, two of the living-room windows have been boarded up with plywood. From the inside, I see two gaping, jagged holes in the glass. Someone has cleaned up, but there is still dried blood on the edges of the holes. The carpet just below the window shows new blood stains, which will now begin their assimilation into the surrounding mottle.

I feel ashamed of my cowardice, sorry that I missed the climax of the drama, and glad I didn't have to see it.

Alvin is the group leader today. I'm feeling slightly confident. I tell the group I called my old workplace and it went okay. I didn't say anything crazy to my boss. He told me they're still holding my job open for me. I don't understand why he's being so nice.

A group member asks me what my job was. I'm nervous talking about this. I start forcing words out. I say I was a foreign-student advisor at an English language school. I helped students with immigration issues, led outings to local tourist attractions, met people from all over the world. I even taught a few class sessions.

Alvin breaks in.

"You sound like you think you're pretty hot shit."

I stare at him.

"Nothing smells quite like hot shit," he says.

I am flooded with confusing emotions. I feel guilty that I've ever had a job when some of the people in this room have spent most of their lives sick and medicated. I don't want to make them feel bad, but I'm terrified that I've become one of them. I want to prove I'm not. And I feel superior because of my past accomplishments.

"You puff yourself up like a balloon—that balloon's gonna burst. You're heading for a relapse."

Relapse!

"Well, what do you expect me to do?" I ask him. "I'm supposed to try to get back to work, aren't I?"

"Now you're whining," Alvin says. "There's just two ways I've ever heard you talk in here. You're either bragging or you're whining."

He's nailed me again. I always feel like I'm either forcing out phony bravado or acting like a wimp.

"But what—what am I supposed to do?"

I look at him, pleading for an answer.

"You expect me to tell you what to do? You keep that up and what? Maybe I'm going to grow boobs so you can start sucking on my tit?"

He moves his hand to his chest, cupping an imaginary breast.

The next day I tell Dr. Leighter what Alvin said about relapse. Dr. Leighter says I'm doing fine.

"A lot of therapists don't know what they're talking about," he says.

Joanna also helps me feel better when I tell her about Alvin. She says there's some jerk at her workplace she doesn't like either. She calls him "the bane of my existence." I tell her Alvin is the bane of mine.

Despite help from Dr. Leighter and Joanna, the suggestion of relapse chills me to my core. I do not want to go back to Room 262, or whatever Room 262 looks like at Western State. Sometimes it seems that's exactly where I'm headed.

A misty rain is falling and I'm on the bus, going nowhere in particular. I look out the window and the weirdness comes on. Everyone is walking with a slight limp, hitching one leg past the other like broken toys. The bus slides by a mob of people waiting at a bus shelter. Their clothing is normal. Shirts buttoned up to necks, hair and hats on top of heads. But their facial features are gone. Noses, mouths, and eyes are replaced by blank flesh, like a thigh has been transplanted where the face should be.

My adrenaline spikes and my heart races. But the terror thrill lasts only a second. I look around. No one's face has changed on the bus. I look back out the window at the bus stop—same old reality. They have their faces back.

That afternoon, I join a basketball game at the SMHI gym. The teams are made up of patients and staff members. As I dribble the ball up the court, I feel dizzy. I curse my meds but keep going. I'm trying to have faith. The dizziness fades the more I move up and down the court. At one point, I score a basket.

"Nice shot!" yells Jane.

She's just trying to encourage me, I think. *But wait—that's negative thinking.*

"Thanks!" I yell back, trying to mix in some positive self-esteem with the faith.

A few minutes later my ankle starts to feel weak.

Damnit. Everything was going so well. And now this.

I take a break, tighten my shoes and return to the game. My ankle feels fine.

All I needed to do was re-tie my shoes. There never was a physical problem.

But I still feel weak and shaky.

Then it hits me—I've committed a terrible spiritual error. By complaining, I doubted. I let my faith slip.

Jesus can't work his miracles when people doubt.

All my confidence and energy drain away. The gym is loud and echoing.

"*Oh, ye of little faith…*" Jesus said.

I avoid Jane's encouraging looks, leave the game, drag myself back to my room, and write in my journal.

Can such severe punishment come from just a single doubt?

"I had a bad hallucination yesterday," I say to Dr. Leighter in our next session. I go on to describe the bus-stop incident. When he questions me about it in more detail, I realize that maybe the people's missing faces were obscured in the shadow of the bus shelter.

He says I had suffered a momentary *illusion*.

"There's a difference between an illusion and a hallucination," he says. "Your mind didn't invent something that wasn't there, you misinterpreted something real. Just ignore stuff like that. You've been in the halfway house a month and you're doing fine."

"But what if that happens again?"

"Look, no more thinking there's some twilight zone conspiracy against you. No more brooding about modern physics," he says. "Concentrate on Joe and on the practical matters of life, like going back to work, getting places on time."

It feels like he's chastising me, but I also pick up the implication that he believes I'm capable of doing what he says.

"You need to stop philosophizing and existentializing, and once in a while stop and smell the flowers."

That same afternoon, Jane tells me I need to "lighten up."

I go for a walk. The gray sidewalk clomps along at my feet. Grass pokes through the mud on the parking strip, which slides by on my right. Some stumpy trees are coming along on my left, leaning over into the sidewalk space, offering their pink buds. They're not exactly flowers and I don't smell them.

But they do look nice.

I'm at my mom's house for the afternoon. She hands me a letter from CARE, thanking me for my generous donation of $250. My check finally got through. They've also included several glossy brochures requesting more money.

Geez, don't they know I've been through "spend-down status"?

I go up to the park near my parents' house for a jog. I start trotting around the dirt path that circles the reservoir in the center of the park. On one side of the path are dark woods. On the other is a ten-foot chain link fence, with barbed wire around the top. Through the fence I can see the blue water.

I'm aware of the rosary hanging around my neck and I start praying desperately. It's cold and windy, and there's no one around.

"Please heal me!" I yell out into the wind. "Dear God, please heal me!"

I grab at the rosary and pull the cross on the end of it out into the wind. As I beg and plead, I clutch the cross, fearful and doubting and slightly hoping. I'm also crushing it in anger.

Tears run down my cheeks, burning in the wind. I struggle to keep up a jogging pace, to not slump back into slow walking. I pull air into my lungs. Again, I sense that putting out energy is threatening, that I'm opening myself up for a fall. As I plant one foot in front of the other, will the ground hold? Or will the ground and I collapse?

A message comes to me, an inner whisper from the glowing presence I sensed in the hospital.

"You will be given back all that was taken from you."

I have a tough time believing this, but somewhere within me the words settle in. Some of my fear drains away. My pace becomes less forced and I lope along for a while.

I'm still pissed. Why can't it all be given back to me right now?

But I go home and write the promise into my journal:

"You will be given back all that was taken from you."

FIFTEEN
Moving Along

Nick's "acting out," as the staff calls it, earns him a trip to the ER and then back to the mental ward. Within a week, he returns to the Inn. His forearms are wrapped in bandages and the marks on his face are still healing, but he's calm. I wonder if it's the same for him as it was for me in the hospital: The pressure built up inside him and had to bust out so he could start over.

One evening, out on the front porch, Nick tells me they let him leave the hospital when he finally convinced them he was "no longer suicidal."

"But that's bullshit," Nick says. "I wasn't trying to kill myself. I flipped out and smashed a couple of windows. There was a lot of blood, but I didn't intend to hurt myself—I didn't even know what I was doing."

I tell Nick about Dr. Hardaway insisting that my mere 15-foot jump from the bathroom window was a suicide attempt.

"Psychiatrists have suicide on the brain," he says.

"Yeah. They ever give you Haldol?"

"No. But I've had plenty of Thorazine."

"Haldol really fucked me up," I say. "The shakes. I didn't take a crap for two weeks. But I've heard Thorazine is worse."

"It's pretty bad," says Nick. "And then the meds they give you for the side effects have even more side effects."

I laugh.

It feels good, sharing war stories.

Talent show night arrives. The TV has been moved and everyone is crammed into chairs facing the "stage." We watch an earnest singer and a puppet act. I'm next up as a resident named Tom goes on.

In regular life, Tom has a lot of jerky, manic energy. He's the guy who is always cackling at the TV, no matter what's on. But I like the way he pumps laughing gas into almost any conversation. For the show Tom needs only to turn this up a notch and he's got an act. He races onstage, wrapped in a bed sheet, giggling maniacally. He produces a slew of toilet paper rolls, holds each by one end and throws them over the heads of the audience. The paper unspools as the rolls fly through the air. Tom's act makes no sense, but it's very popular. Everyone except the heavily medicated residents whoops and cheers. Steven stands at the back frowning, with his arms folded. I figure he's pissed off that Tom has raided the supply closet.

It's a tough act to follow. I take a deep breath, step forward and start juggling. This is the first time I've performed in front of a real audience since I went crazy. I drop once, but I do fine.

Lars calls for a family counseling session. My dad and mom and I meet with him in a small office on the SMHI campus. Lars throws out random questions about family history or a typical family interaction as he gestures with his unlit pipe.

"How does this family solve conflict?" he asks.

We all agree that there isn't much conflict in our family.

"Everyone gets along fine," one of us says. The others nod.

I see Lars smirking and wonder if my parents notice.

"All right," he says. "Let's talk about next steps. Joe's moving along in our program here and the Inn is supposed to be temporary housing. Where might Joe go next?"

"He's welcome to come back home," Dad says.

Secretly, I know I'd go crazy all over again if I had to live back with my parents right now. But I can't explain why.

"I couldn't stand to go back to that room I freaked out in," I say. "And there are renters on the third floor."

"We could set you up in a basement room," says my dad. He continues to calmly work on the problem, but my mom looks anxious and concerned.

After my parents leave, Lars asks me a question:

"Have you seen your dad like that very often?"

"Like what?" I say. I think about the stuff Dad said. "He's the same. I know he wants what's best for me."

"I mean sitting still in a chair like that, talking to you about stuff that really matters," Lars says.

Wow.

In this moment, I experience a profound shift. Lars seems to be criticizing my dad for never taking the time to sit down and talk with me.

No one criticizes my dad. There's nothing to criticize him for. Dad doesn't have flaws. Sure, I got angry with him from time to time over the years, but I always concluded that I was the problem. Dad is hardworking and busy and calm and competent and does everything the right way. I am irrational, frustrated, and incompetent.

But now—in a flash—I realize that maybe Dad kept himself *too* busy. Even when he was home from work he was always up in his office paying bills or out in the shop. Dad spent time with the family at dinner, but as soon as the meal was over, he called for the newspaper and started reading. He did a ton of hands-on volunteer work. And if any of us ever needed help moving or fixing a car or something, Dad's mantra was "I'm available."

He was "there for me," but he was too busy for me.

The only time we were ever alone together sitting down was in the car. That's when I'd hesitantly seek fatherly advice or try to discuss some deeper aspect of life.

"Do you really believe all the stuff the church teaches?" I asked him once as we were driving along.

"Yes," he said, without further comment.

I look at Lars.

"You're right. Dad barely ever talks to me like that. It's just really weird for me to hear you point it out. I've never seen my dad as having any flaws."

"Dad is a hero to most boys growing up," says Lars. "I used to idealize my father, too, but he's just a human being, making his way through life like everybody else."

I start making friends with Ken. He's more intelligent than his part-time catatonia would indicate. I wonder how much of his flat, monotone voice is him and how much is the meds. And I wonder if my meds change how others see me.

Ken says that despite his problems, he thinks he's getting better. This gives me a feeling that there's hope for some of us, but I wonder if his bizarre behavior means he'll become a chronic. I don't want either one of us to yield to the temptation to permanently slip away into the craziness.

One day I ask Ken, "What's going on when you stand out there on the parking strip?"

"Sometimes I just need things to be quiet and still," he says.

For a few days, I'm sick with the flu and I don't seem to be getting well. I go into the office and tell Steven, "I'm thinking I'll go to my parents' house for a few days so I can get better."

"So Mommy can nursemaid you?" Steven asks.

He's a half-foot shorter than me. His sharp face pokes up at me.

"No…" I say.

"You do that, and we'll discharge you," he says.

Steven is looking down at some papers on his desk. I'm dismissed.

I complain about this to Bella.

Bella says, "They couldn't get away with treating us like that if we weren't mental patients."

Later a nicer staff member explains to me that state regulations require the Inn to discharge a patient who spends more than one night away. Why couldn't Steven have just told me that?

Nick and I are hanging out on the front porch. He tells me that last night Tom jumped off an overpass onto the freeway. They took him to the emergency room, where he died.

Although I didn't know Tom well, this is a shock. I had heard about a resident who had jumped off the Aurora Bridge just before I moved in, but even with all the talk about suicide and the random attempts, Tom is the only guy I've known who successfully offed himself.

Nick blames Steven and the mental health bureaucracy for shuffling Tom around until he ended up homeless and hopeless.

"He refused to go to substance abuse treatment, so Steven told him to go sleep under a bridge."

"More of Steven's bullshit," I say. "And this time it was fatal."

"Tom came to visit me every day in the hospital after I smashed out those windows," Nick says.

I feel guilty that I never visited Nick. I also worry about the effect living amongst all this carnage has on my mental health.

SIXTEEN
SEEMING NORMAL

I'm worried about Ken because he keeps getting up and walking out of group therapy to go stand on the parking strip. If he gets kicked out of group, he gets kicked out of Day Treatment, and if he gets kicked out of Day Treatment, he gets kicked out of the Inn. There aren't many places for a guy like Ken to go.

In group one day, Ken raises his hand.

"You don't have to raise your hand," Alvin reminds him.

"Alvin, I'm going to have to leave soon," says Ken.

"We have 20 more minutes," says Alvin.

"I can't stay," says Ken.

"You can't be in group if you can't stay."

Ken lifts himself up off his chair for a moment, then sits down.

"Tell us what's goin' on, Ken," Alvin says.

"I just can't sit here."

"That's your choice. What does the group think Ken should do?"

"Stay," says Nick.

"I'd like him to stay," says Bella.

"So would I," I say.

A few minutes later Ken suddenly bolts upright in his chair. He stands up and walks out the door.

I turn to Alvin.

"Can I go talk to him?"

"Go ahead," he says.

I catch Ken walking down one of the pathways toward the street.

"Hey, man," I say.

Ken turns slowly toward me. He looks very calm. Frozen.

"I can't sit there," he says.

"They're going to kick you out."

"I know."

"If you get kicked out, you have to leave the Inn."

"I know."

We stand there a while. Ken is his upright self. He has excellent posture.

"Come on," I say. "You can do it."

He follows me back and takes his seat, knees sticking out, back stiff, leaning forward in his chair, until group is finally over.

Ken shocks everyone by leaving the Inn in favor of the Holy Grail: independent housing. His brother has leased a house six blocks from the Inn and he rents Ken a basement room for a price he can manage on his welfare stipend. But Ken still shows up to Day Treatment, tolerating Alvin's ongoing jabs.

Ken invites me over to his place to play music. He stands straight and stiff and woodenly strums a white electric guitar. He's pretty good at keeping rhythm. I chime in on harmonica. I never could play very well, but it's fun.

The next day, I'm at my parents' house for lunch and I tell my mom about playing music with Ken. She frowns. I think she's worried I'm hanging out with the mentally ill too much.

One day in late May, two months after I've arrived at the Inn, I tell the group I've talked to my old boss on the phone again. He says I can come back anytime I feel ready.

"So I'm going to try to go back to work in a couple of weeks," I say.

"Okay, Joe," Lars says. "Try to get out of that chair."

I stand up. He gestures for me to sit down.

"No, don't get up from the chair. Just *try* to get up."

I get the point. I sit there "trying," feeling the straining effort in my rigid muscles.

Later, as I work on this lesson from Lars, I see that I have been held back by a subconscious mental image of myself "trying" to go back to work. I'm cowering behind a tree, trying to get up the nerve to approach the building. I replace that with the picture of myself walking semi-confidently through the front door.

Ken is also making progress. He hasn't been out on the parking strip for weeks and he's ready to graduate from Day Treatment. When I was in the hospital, I was jealous when other patients had success and were discharged, but I find myself rooting for Ken. Although I can still fall prey to the notion that I'm not getting any better, I no longer see someone else's success as proof that I'm a big loser.

Part of the graduation process entails listening to the therapists' contradictory instructions for how we should see ourselves. On the one hand, we have a "mental illness," which is nothing to be ashamed of. We take medicine for it, as if we have the flu or heart disease. We shouldn't think of ourselves as inferior, inherently flawed, morally bankrupt, or possessed by demons.

On the other hand, transitioning back into regular society is strictly a stealth operation. The therapists coach us to keep our histories and current situation a secret when dealing with normal people.

"There's a stigma. People don't understand, so it's best to keep this private," they tell us. We should prepare a cover story for when we meet any potential friend, lover, or employer, and avoid going into details.

"You need to get to know people well before you trust them," Jane tells us.

My alibi hasn't changed since I went into the hospital: "A bad case of Montezuma's revenge."

My fear increases when Nick tells me that, despite five years of a spotless record with his former employer, they turned him down for re-hire when they found out about his mental health history. He hasn't found work since.

I'm terrified that returning to my former job is my one and only chance.

"Role Playing" appears on the group schedule. I remember the improvisation class I took the previous year at the University of Washington. I had performed well, soaking in the laughter and applause. But that seems like a long time ago.

The theme for Role Playing is "self-assertion." I hesitantly volunteer for a scene in which a teenage son is arguing with his mother about curfew. Jane plays the mother.

"I want you home at 11," she whines up at me.

I take a breath. I haven't put out the energy this requires since I went nuts. Everyone is watching.

"I want you home at 11!" Jane says again.

"No, Mom…"

My voice sounds like someone else talking. I shiver.

"No, Mom… I'm coming home at midnight."

I croak out a few more objections and the role play ends. I sit down in my chair, hyperventilating. I catch my breath.

That wasn't so bad.

I'm talking with my brother Tim at my parents' house. He tells me he's seen my roommate, Ronnie, running around Volunteer Park like a maniac.

"If he doesn't settle down, he's going to get arrested."

I feel protective of Ronnie, and embarrassed, like Ronnie is out in society representing all of us wackos at the Inn.

I go back and find Ronnie in our room.

"You doing okay?" I ask.

"I'm fine," says Ronnie. "Hee hee hee."

I offer him some free advice.

"You know, that paint sniffing can damage your brain."

"Don't worry," he says. "I don't do that no more."

I start going over to St. Joseph's church for Mass at noon on weekdays. It gives me something to do and it's quiet. I also secretly hope I'm making up for my sins.

"I notice you're not taking communion," Father Carroll says to me one day after the service.

It's true. They always told us you're not supposed to take communion with sin on your soul. Not that I have some major sin I'm especially worried about. I've had the deep talks with Patricia and I've been to confession with Father Carroll. But I still feel too overall guilty, too messed-up.

In fifth grade they taught us about sin and what it does to your soul. I pictured my soul as a wavering gelatinous membrane that floated throughout my chest and belly. With each sin, a dark ragged hole appears. My soul still feels like blackened Swiss cheese.

Father Carroll touches my arm.

"Joe, we don't take communion because we deserve it. We take it because we need it."

He fills me in on some church history. In the centuries prior to Vatican II, the church discouraged parishioners from taking communion. But that's changed.

"Jesus wants us to take communion," he says. "It's a way he gives us strength and comfort."

I like the idea of Jesus wanting me to take communion. This sounds friendly and inviting. But I don't want Father Carroll to think I'm returning to communion just because he told me to, so I wait until a different priest is saying Mass. I march up and hold out my cupped hands and take the host. I place it on my tongue and walk slowly back to the pew. The lump of host has a warm glow as it makes its way down my throat. It feels good to believe I have taken in something from a healing source.

I tell Dr. Leighter about the self-assertion role play and subsequent ones that went even better.

"It felt sort of like my old improvisation class," I tell him.

Dr. Leighter proposes his own role-play exercise.

"I want you to choose your favorite movie star. Get some clothes like he would wear and then go downtown and talk with people as if you are him."

I pick Humphrey Bogart. The fedora and trench coat would be over the top, but I get a tie and my dark suit jacket from my parents' house. I board a bus heading downtown and flash my bus pass. As I start walking down the aisle, I realize that others on the bus have no way of knowing I live at a halfway house, or that their taxes just paid my bus fare. I put a bit of swagger in my step. I'm Bogart.

Downtown, I stroll around, practicing my confident walk, but I can't screw up my courage enough to talk to anyone. I'd like to buy lunch and talk to a waitress, but I can't afford it. I go into a drug store to buy a pack of gum. I exchange friendly words with the matronly clerk. I'm not trying to talk in Bogart's voice—that would be ridiculous—but while we're chatting, I open the gum and plop a piece in my mouth the suave way Bogart would handle a cigarette. I bid the clerk a hearty goodbye.

I go for broke. I walk into Nordstrom in search of a pretty girl. I spot a cute blonde close to my age at the cosmetics counter. My legs shake a bit as I approach. I remind myself that Bogart has no fear of women.

The girl and I have a pleasant five-minute chat. The few things I say about myself are based on my previous life, which I pretend is what's happening now. She looks right into my eyes and I look right into hers. Some of my old energy for chatting up girls comes back.

Wow, it's still there.

I spend an evening with my old friend Pete at his apartment watching a Sonics game. I cheer for Lenny Wilkens, my boyhood basketball hero, who now coaches the team. Then I notice something unusual. The entire evening has gone by and I haven't noticed anything unusual.

Just a couple of guys watching the game, I think, as I take a swig from my bottle of 7up.

Despite my inarguable improvement, the weirdness refuses to take a permanent vacation. The next evening I walk the seven blocks from the Inn to my aunt's house, feeling nervous for no reason. I spot tiny alien plants poking up out of my aunt's lawn, hundreds of them. I bend down and look closer. Each weird little leaf is glowing green and drips with unnatural-looking water from the recent rain.

Is that heavy water?

I'm remembering a modern physics term.

What is heavy water?

My aunt Jean welcomes me at the door, wiping her hands on a dirty apron. She ushers me into the front room, where my grandfather knocks his pipe loudly against his massive copper ashtray, blackened with decades of soot. When we were kids he sat in that same chair, watching football all Sunday, ignoring us, wearing giant white headphones.

My mother, Joanna, and two of my brothers are also here, making polite conversation. Their laughs sound phony. My grandfather coughs into his big blue cowboy handkerchief. He's not a cowboy, but he owns some rifles, lodged in a rack above his bed. He's an outdoorsman like my father. They are real men.

I walk into the kitchen and see that Grandpa has made his famous hamburger recipe.

When I was a boy, my grandfather and my aunt sure knew how to host a hamburger feast. My mom made hamburgers out of 100% meat, but my grandfather mixed in an egg, onions, and hunks of old bread, making his burgers supremely plump and delicious. Tonight, however,

I am convinced that the desperate flotsam of his recipe is clearly the product of a mind deranged by the deprivations of the Depression.

Things get worse when we're seated eating dinner. I notice an oil-company calendar on the wall. It features a snowy scene. But it's not this year's calendar. Who would keep an outdated calendar? I gasp inwardly as my head swivels left and I see another old calendar. This one features a Norman Rockwell painting of a medical professional embarrassing a child. Yet another calendar shows a fire truck. I try to keep cool as my eyes whip around the kitchen, counting no fewer than seven wall calendars from different years.

I'm deep in the twilight zone again. None of this can be real: the sprouts in the lawn, the bizarre hoard of calendars. I work hard to "maintain," avoiding eye contact. There are too many people here.

If anyone notices I'm acting weird, they don't say anything.

I finish dinner, decline a ride, and hurry along the dark streets back to the halfway house. I'm on the walkway leading toward the front porch when a recently admitted resident stops me.

"Why doesn't anyone ever talk to you here?" he asks me.

I look at him. His unkempt hair is haloed in the streetlight. It fires off in all directions.

"No one ever talks to you here," he says again.

Is he trying to freak me out? *Some* people talk to me. *He's* talking to me. I don't want to talk to him.

"I don't know, man," I say and keep going.

Odette is the only one on the porch. She's staring off into space. At the end of her hand, her cigarette ignores her. Another lost soul in Hell.

In bed, it's old-home week for the repetitive crazy loops:

And now the screaming starts.

You made your bed, now lie in it.

As I lie there I realize that my punishment from here on is that I will never be allowed another night's sleep. I shortly tire of this and fall asleep.

In the morning, I wake up feeling deeply ashamed. I have an appointment with Dr. Leighter in the afternoon. I lie in bed, imagining how disappointed he will be if I go in and torture him with my tale of last night's visit to Hell. I have been doing so well, racking up chunks of feeling-normal time.

I reflect on last night and try to think about it in ways that will please Dr. Leighter. There was something sprouting out of my aunt's lawn. Well, it's springtime. Things sprout.

But that many things?

Alien things?

Dr. Leighter said, "You learn something new every day." Maybe there are just a lot of lucky seedlings this year.

So my aunt has a bunch of calendars. Maybe her collection is eccentric. So what? It's her house. Maybe she likes the artwork. It's not my problem or my business.

> *Last night, in honor of the full moon, I went crazy again. I thought I was in Hell. Very shook up. I thought everything at Jean's house was absurd. Nobody noticed my extreme paranoia. It wasn't until this morning that it occurred to me that nothing was really that wild.*
>
> —Journal entry, May 1979

Joanna stops by and we take a walk around the neighborhood.

"Did I seem normal last night at Aunt Jean's?" I ask her.

"Yeah."

"I wasn't. I was barely holding it together."

"Well, you fooled me," she says.

"Maybe a part of being sane is pretending to be sane when you feel insane," I say.

"Good point, Joseph," she says.

SEVENTEEN
HAPPY TRAILS

A bunch of us residents are clustered in groups on the front porch of the Inn. I'm sitting in a chair. Nick and Bella sit across from me. Bella says something and takes a drag on her cigarette.

Suddenly, for no reason, the perceptual shift comes upon me. It's instantaneous, just like in the hospital. The lighting goes stark and harsh, the shadows deepen, and every flaw on Bella's face snaps into high relief. I see each acne scar and blemish and even her clean hair looks greasy. Nick's eye sockets deepen. The movements of the other residents around me become jerky. A dark shadow has slashed across the porch.

Wow, it's happening again.

But this time, it's as if I'm watching a horror movie. I know it's not real. I'm just sitting in my seat. I know this is still Nick and Bella. She keeps talking and smoking.

Just hang on. Everything's okay.

The effect soon passes and all returns to normal.

The perceptual shift never happens again.

Lars and I are walking the winding pathways of the SMHI campus. Several chronics sit on the benches, including Andy, who sports a long gray beard. His body shakes with a ghostly tremor. Even his beard shakes.

I'm grinding away again on how far from grace I've fallen.

"My ego has been completely crushed," I say.

"No, you still think well of yourself. If you didn't you wouldn't be taking my time. You keep trying to get better."

I flash back to my time in the hospital and see that this energy, sometimes revved-up, sometimes dormant, has always been in me. Even my escape attempts were an expression of this inner determination.

"I can tell you what your problem is," Lars says.

"What?"

"You can't *move on* from where you are until you *accept* where you are. Stop comparing yourself to what you have been or what you could be. Stop fighting what is. Accept what you are now."

He concludes with another Lars zinger:

"Are you planning to spend the next 30 years saying, 'Boy, that sure was unfair what happened to me back in 1979'?"

That afternoon I'm writing in my journal. I look around our room. As usual, it's trashed: clothes everywhere, the meager possessions of two insane welfare bums spread out where we can lay our hands on them any time we want them.

Ronnie is sitting on his bed, babbling along to his radio. At my insistence it's on low volume and at his it's set to talk radio.

"Yeah, mister…" he is saying. "Hee hee hee hee."

His pants are splattered with new paint stains.

I live in a place where the inmates don't bathe for weeks. The meat loaf comes in shades of green. My friend put his arm through the living-room window. Tom killed himself leaping onto the freeway.

I start to write down what Lars said. I look at my left hand. It's moving across the page as I write. Blue ink emerges out the tip of my pen as I solidly push each word out, one after another.

You can't move on unless you accept where you are. Accept what you are now.

Late in the afternoon, I go back across the street determined to give Lars' acceptance idea a shot. I ask William, one of the counselors, if he'll play some basketball.

He smiles and says, "Sure."

William is a jovial, rotund black guy a few years older than me, and two or three inches shorter. I don't have the kind of deep talks with him that I have with Lars, but William has an open, positive presence, a spirit he offers to everyone, including the most severely ailing chronics. Lars and Alvin tend to expend their talents with the more functioning members of our cadre.

William and I walk into the deserted gym and agree to play a game to seven points. One-on-one is the most exhausting form of basketball and I'm afraid of running out of breath.

I'm in such horrible shape, I think.

Then, with Lars' words in mind, I replace that with:

That's the shape you're in. Accept it.

William lets me have the ball first. I've watched him play before, so I know he's no superstar. He plays at about the same mediocre level I used to, which means he should cream me today. I start to dribble around him to the left and toss up a shot. It goes in! Good start.

We trade misses and baskets for a while. He's ahead, but he's not wiping me out. And, although he's smiling, I can tell from all his huffing and puffing he's really trying.

Suddenly, my muscles feel weak, and I'm dizzy.

Goddamn it. Those damn meds are taking me down.

I accept that I'm on meds. I take a few breaths.

William throws up a shot that misses the rim and the backboard. I grab the ball.

Damn. He's not even as good as I used to be. I should be beating him easily. Except that I'm crippled by being insane and weak and a loser.

I accept that I am insane and weak and a loser.

The score is now five to six, with William one basket from winning. I'm exhausted. I resolve to try a tricky shot I used to be able to make — the turn-around fade-away jumper. Dribbling with your back to the hoop, you jump up with a twist, turning toward the basket in the air. I'm not sure I can even attempt it with William's girth bouncing off me. I take a deep breath, leap, and throw up the shot. Score! We're tied six to six.

I don't recall who won the game, but that afternoon I won a big chunk of my sanity back.

> *Instead of being all pissed off because I couldn't play nearly as good as I used to, I resolved simply to play as well as I could with the skills I now possess. It worked.*
>
> —Letter to a friend, May 1979

I'm heading back to my job for the first time since before I left for Mexico. I'm five months late for work.

I'm scheduled from 10:00 a.m. to noon. I'm embarrassed by the short shift and that I'm coming back as a lowly audio lab assistant. But my boss has assured me I can return to my previous job as a student advisor when I get more comfortable.

This is my one and only chance to claw my way back to the working world.

I walk up the curving drive toward the entrance. When I escaped from the hospital I intended to come up here and hurl myself from an open window on the tenth floor.

Paul, my boss, greets me in the lobby and shakes my hand. He seems to be looking at me a little too deeply. I imagine he's trying to figure out if I'm still crazy. But he still has his graying beard and soft blue eyes, which give me comfort.

We walk past the main office. A quick glance through the door unnerves me. I spot one of the teachers I always wanted to sleep with, as well as a teacher who always wanted to sleep with me. And there's Chuck, who was mentoring me in learning how to teach.

I'm within a four-dimensional web, woven out of the strands of all the social relationships I've had with people in this building: teachers, administrators, students. The sight of each person jerks me back into a story that was in progress, a story abruptly put on pause for five months.

Paul and I make our way to the audio lab, a large room with rows of individual listening stations. The master control desk rises up in the front like a judge's bench, where the audio lab supervisor manages a bank of cassette tapes.

Mahmoud, a good friend and co-worker, is joining me for the shift. For two years, we lead student activities together, including co-hosting two boisterous talent shows. He gives me a big smile. I feel like a shadow of the fellow he used to know.

I'm startled to remember him telling me about the brutality of the wars that have torn apart his homeland, Lebanon. I was once able to talk about such horrors and not feel overwhelmed.

I distribute study packets to the students as Mahmoud offers instructions from the front of the room. Weaving among the aisles, I am pleased to find I am capable of getting a student a pencil.

I sense myself shifting from the role of mental patient to that of a paid worker with tasks that must be done. But I also feel like I'm walking around inside a fragile bubble that barely keeps all this stimulation from crashing in on me.

I return to the front of the room and help Mahmoud load tapes. Suddenly, the cassette in my hand shudders as I watch the brown ribbon of tape pass right through its white plastic guides. Quantum physics is on the loose again. I just saw a substance pass through a solid surface. The tape is flopping around outside of the cassette. I panic. And I'm angry at God that something weird is happening, today of all days. Deep inside I send up this prayer:

Help!

I hyperventilate. I look over and see Mahmoud writing something. If I talk to him he might say something bizarre. The sea of students before me undulates.

I look down at the tape again.

From deep within, the silent inner voice coaches me on the fundamentals of my rebuilt sanity.

It's okay.

Accept where you are.

Check it out.

Somehow my eyes focus on the line where the top and bottom sections of the plastic cassette are joined. I see a tiny gap, which is how the tape ribbon slipped through. The panic sucks back inside me, like a wave subsiding, gathering itself.

You checked it out. Everything is okay.

A depressing thought rushes in:

Can't you even do the easiest job in the school without messing up?

I push at the tape, and it eases back through the gap. I put a finger in each of the holes to tighten the cassette, as I've done many times before. I let out a breath.

I can do this.

This mini-drama, from madness attack through the re-gathering of my sanity, spirit, and confidence, takes less than a minute.

The rest of my shift is uneventful. When I say goodbye to Mahmoud, he shakes my hand and says he'll see me tomorrow at 10.

I'm invited to the bachelor party of a high school friend from the old neighborhood. Pete picks me up at the Inn and drives us to meet the rest of the guys at a neighborhood tavern. It's a small group, just six of us.

I marvel at how normal it all is. I get the jokes. I even tell one of my own. It's like the old days, a group of guys having a few beers. I keep my alcohol consumption in check because of the meds, but I love joining in.

The guys decide to trundle down to a neighborhood girlie bar. We park and walk down a quiet street toward the club. The evening has cooled. Trees with dark branches reach up, offering spring leaves in silhouette. Cars go by, headlights softly cutting the night air. Everyone is talking and laughing.

The club is tacky but cozy, with soft, multi-colored lights. Waitresses stop by in tight T-shirts, and half-dressed girls dance on the stage. But I don't stare at them. I'm basking in the exquisite miracle of bland normalcy: an evening with the guys, the trees, the girls, the beers, the passing cars, the jokes, the stage lights, the cool of the night.

Pete drops me off at the halfway house. There's a bounce in my walk as I go up the front steps. I wonder if Pete appreciates the literary, romantic quality of his old pal living here.

I am living in a flophouse, I think. *Something Kerouac or Jack London would do.*

I go to my room and climb into bed. Ronnie is quiet tonight. All is well. The next day I write in my journal:

> *"Don's bachelor party is the first social evening out when I felt normal the <u>entire time</u>."*

Perhaps it's the less-than-sanitary conditions at the Inn, but my lymphedema catches up with me and I get a leg infection. I realize that I'll never recover at the Inn, so I move to my parents' house.

I hate being sick, but this is a great test of my fledgling sanity. I decide against living in the basement and take the same room where I believed I had passed into the realm of the dead so many months prior. Living at Mom and Dad's turns out to be no big deal. The weirdness that haunted me there during my initial freak-out, and in so many subsequent visits, has evaporated. My parents still sometimes bug me, but I know that would be the case for any guy in his twenties who is back living with his parents.

As per Steven's threat, I'm discharged from the Inn for being away too many nights. But I continue at SMHI.

In June 1979, at my very last therapy group, the staff leads us in a graduation tradition I have witnessed many times. Therapists and patients hold hands in a circle and sing "Happy Trails" in honor of the graduate. This time, that's me.

"Happy trails to you, until we meet again.
Happy trails to you, keep smiling until then."

The therapists sing this with a big dose of irony, particularly on Alvin's part. It's a ritual that has always seemed dumb to me. But now, as I look around the circle, a sense of goodness and satisfaction hovers beneath my cynicism. Nick and Bella and Audrey and the others are wishing me well. Jane and Lars are smiling and nodding.

"Some trails are happy ones, others are blue.
It's the way you ride the trail that counts, here's a happy one for you."

Nobody knows these ending lyrics except the therapists, but we all do our best to sing along.

EIGHTEEN
PARALLEL WORLDS

*I feel I've been through hell and survived. I have thought I was
in HELL. I have thought I was Dead. Turns out not to be true.
Turns out that God is here right now, loving me as I love those
around me. I have been almost totally w/o love. Now the love
(like) between me and Ronnie and me and Bella is very
valuable to me.*

—Journal entry, June 1979

Waking up sane each morning in my parents' house, I feel like Dorothy
at the end of *The Wizard of Oz*—slightly stunned by what I have survived
but grateful to have returned to reality. The July sun shines on the green
leaves that brush against my bedroom window. I glimpse a powerful
truth: Sanity is a glorious gift.

I still fear relapse, and from time to time the weirdness creeps in if
I'm under stress, but increasingly I'm able to shake it off. I've continued
to see Dr. Leighter for follow-up care, and he urges me to focus on the
fundamentals. I talk to Pete and he agrees to share an apartment with
me starting August 1. My boss schedules me to resume full-time work
in September. I'll be able to pay my rent.

But an empty July looms ahead. Although I often see friends in the
evenings, I know that spending my days wandering around my parents'
house, staring at the walls or the television, will not be good for me.
It occurs to me that my story of mental illness and recovery could be
a feature article for the *Seattle Times* Sunday magazine. I still know some
editors at the paper.

I bring my tape recorder and reporter's notebook to one of my therapy sessions with Dr. Leighter. The role of journalist gives me a framework for reviewing our work together, but below the surface, I have conflicting emotions. I feel grateful. I've often told others "he saved my life." But I'm nervous because I plan to talk to him about a time I think he made a mistake.

"What was my diagnosis?" I ask him.

"Dr. Hardaway felt that you were suffering from psychotic depression with paranoid features."

Yeah, I guess I was a paranoid psycho, I think, *but it's rough to hear myself summed up like that.*

"Did you think that was correct?"

"You were psychotic, in the sense that you were out of touch with reality."

"Like thinking I was going to be tortured?"

"Yes, but after I had treated you for a couple of weeks," he says, "I wasn't certain that the diagnosis of psychosis was still valid. I thought a trial period without the antidepressant might be a good idea. But you were not able to tolerate that."

This is what I want to ask him about and it's come up without warning. The memory is still fresh: He's erasing the order for Navane as I stand there sputtering, begging him to taper it off instead.

"Yes, I wish you hadn't taken me off so quick—all at once," I say. My voice is shaking. "That bothered me."

He nods.

"Yes, I recall that within a day or so you were very upset. You believed that this was responsible for an episode of loss of control. Chemically, that's very unlikely, because you would have still had the drug in your system. You had a psychological dependency, and this resulted in a panic reaction."

I see myself strapped to my bed, sweating and screaming.

"Panic? Panic can be that powerful?"

"Oh, yes. When you became extremely frightened, anxiety mounted and mounted to the point where you began to scream and flail until you were uncontrollable. So I began treating you on the basis of severe panic reaction. I put you back on the antidepressant, but you were mostly helped by a lot of reassurance, not medication."

"That's why you kept saying the same things over and over to me?"

I think of his oft-repeated statement: "I like you, Joe, and I believe you're going to get better."

We continue reviewing the details of my craziness, how he helped me, and how I made my way forward.

This conversation boosts my confidence. The diagnosis "depressive paranoid psychosis" sounds like there is something inherently wrong with me. But "severe panic reaction" shifts my self-image to that of a regular guy who became extremely frightened. Everybody gets scared.

I make an appointment to visit Mr. Wiener, the social worker I thought was named after the bloated Polish sausage, the guy who gave me my first mental health assessment a few days after I got back from my Mexico trip.

I had then perceived him as having bugging eyes, a careening Adam's apple, and sagging face skin. I'm pleased to find that I can recognize his normal self.

"That was a bizarre time for me," I tell him. "I'm wondering what you remember."

"I remember you came in thinking you might be crazy," he says.

I note that the walls of his office are now solid, no longer wavering and melting into yellow sand, like they were five months ago.

"You seemed to be reacting to the difficult breakup you'd had with a young woman."

As he speaks, I listen for the loud gulping sound that had reverberated throughout the office back then. Sure enough, Mr. Wiener has a vocal tic that matches my memory, except the volume now is less than a tenth of what it was then.

"Yeah, I was really upset about that," I say. "But Laurie and I have written each other some nice letters in the last few weeks. We seem to be forgiving each other."

He tells me he's glad I'm feeling better. He strikes me as a nice, caring guy. I see no reason to say anything about his formerly melting face. I shake his hand and leave.

As I walk down the hall, I feel like I've conducted a secret mission, a journey between parallel worlds.

Dr. Hardaway and I meet in a second-floor office off the mental wards. The last time I saw him, I was staggering in and out of psychosis. Dr. Hardaway is wearing his brown three-piece suit. His cuff is still pressed into a blade and he blinks behind the same oversized glasses. But his satanic glow has faded away.

I ask him what he remembers of our time together. He responds with short answers.

"Do you remember that time I stood on your foot?" I ask.

I have a vivid memory of placing my foot on his polished black dress shoe and pressing down as hard as I dared, to see if I could force a human reaction from him.

He pauses.

"Yes. I remember that."

"Why didn't you say anything?"

"I didn't think you knew you were doing it."

Leaving Dr. Hardaway's office, as I head past the 2-North mental ward, I spot Roger, my old nemesis, behind the nurses' station. I hesitate, then walk up to him.

If he's surprised to see me, he doesn't show it.

"I'm just visiting," I say. "Can we talk?"

"Sure," he says.

We step into the meeting area behind the desk and sit down. Roger is the same—sarcastic and skeptical—but I'm different now. I don't feel intimidated or defensive.

Despite the fact that I was in an altered state when I was here before, our memories line up, whether we are discussing group therapy or the wild night I tried to escape out the elevator.

"Do you remember that first night I was here, the night I jumped out the window?" I ask.

"Sure," he says.

"When I woke up, you were sitting next to me."

"We thought it would be wise to keep an eye on you."

I look right at him and plunge ahead.

"Well, it seemed to me that you were making fun of me. You were imitating my mouth movements. Like this."

I demonstrate, making exaggerated puckering and tongue movements.

"My mouth was dry, a side effect of the meds," I say.

"Really?" Roger smiles benignly, like he's used to all the crazy things mental patients say. "No, no, I didn't do that."

"Weird. I have a clear memory of it."

"Well, I might have leaned in to look at you when you woke up. Maybe you misinterpreted something."

Roger sticks with his story. I leave, still not sure what really happened, but glad I brought it up.

On my way out, at the foot of the grand sweeping staircase, I run into Susan and Rene, two of the 2-North nurses I used to think were out to get me. I'm surprised to find it's easy to talk to them. I tell them about the way I used to see the world.

"I'd fixate on weird things like the elevator doors."

"What about them?" asks Rene.

I point down the hall.

"Well, see that elevator has three door panels that slide to the side, but the other one has two panels that open," I say.

"I never noticed that," she says.

"Or look at this staircase, the way it turns at the bottom with three little extra stairs. Like an M.C. Escher painting."

"Yeah, that is a little odd," says Susan.

"Here you are talking about how you don't notice these things anymore, yet you're pointing them out," Rene says with a laugh.

"Well, I just remember them," I say. "I don't notice new ones."

"How did *people* seem to you?" Susan asks.

"Weird and evil. I remember Grace gave me my first dose of Haldol. She had this demonic, sly grin."

"It must have been scary to be feelin' that way," Susan says. Her smile is genuine, but I notice she still drops her g's in that fake, folksy way.

They ask me what helped me get better. I sing the praises of Dr. Leighter and Patricia.

"I have to start a round of meds," says Rene. "I'm so pleased you stopped by."

"I'm glad you don't still think we're evil monsters," says Susan.

"Yes, it's nice to see you are just normal people," I say.

Not to mention cute girls.

I haven't seen Patricia since I left the hospital in early April and I'm excited to show her the sane version of me. We meet for lunch in the hospital cafeteria. I select my old favorites: a tuna sandwich with mashed potatoes and gravy, a hot fudge sundae. I give her the update on my successes with work, housing, friends, and going on a few dates with girls.

"That's tremendous, wonderful," she says.

"I never thought I would get back to the way I was before."

"I know you didn't."

"What was I like in the hospital?"

"You were extremely fearful, suspicious, and guarded," she says. "You were obviously hurting, but it wasn't at all clear what was bothering you."

I'm remembering what a mess I was.

"I know that I didn't want to talk."

"Yes, you were quite resistant to therapy, in a passive-aggressive way."

"I drove Dr. Hardaway crazy."

I hate to admit that my problems with Dr. Hardaway weren't entirely his fault.

"You also did a lot of crappy intellectualization," Patricia says. "But after your suicide attempt, I felt we had to cut to the heart of the matter and start rebuilding your confidence. You would get so angry when I would cut right through your long-winded explanations."

It feels strange to recall the turmoil between us, sitting across from her at a normal lunch. I tell her I appreciate how hard she worked for me.

"Do you remember that time you asked me to let some other patients come upstairs and listen to me play the piano?" I ask.

"Yes, that was one of the nicest times I saw you be part of a group. Each of those patients volunteered to come up there and it was so nice of you to play for them."

"I thought my playing was really bad."

"On the contrary, it was lovely."

"After I played, I heard you tell one of the women that it took a lot of courage for her to come up there. I thought that was an insult directed at me because my playing was so bad it would take courage to listen to it."

"No, she was nervous about any social activities. It did take courage for her to come up there. Yes, it did."

"I know," I say. "I can see that now."

In this moment, my perspective shifts. I now have two parallel memories of this incident. I still vividly recall my paranoid, insecure state, but I also picture what was really going on—she was affirming the woman's bravery.

"I misinterpreted what you said."

"Why didn't you check that out?"

"There are a lot of things I didn't check out."

"Are you getting better at checking? Because I interpret that as a human hurt feeling. If you actually thought I was insulting you, you must have felt hurt. Were you?"

Patricia is drilling in again.

"Yeah."

"Are you getting better at letting your hurts be known?"

"I think so. But I don't interpret things as being against me anymore, the way I used to."

"Are you sure about that?"

I reflect on how paranoid I used to be. I'm not like that now.

"Yes," I say.

"Okay."

I'm embarrassed to imagine Patricia's memories of me at my worst. But it's great to be talking as two sane adults.

Another staff member approaches and starts talking with Patricia. I spot Mike, the guard who captured me after my jump out the window, at another table. I say goodbye to Patricia and bring my tape recorder over to him.

At the time of my jump, I assumed that someone heard me hit the ground and had alerted him. But Mike says his being there was God's providence.

"If the Lord hadn't willed me to be there—I shudder to think what would have happened. I've dealt with many psych patients, as a guard and when I was on the police force, and I've never seen anyone so agitated and determined to do himself in."

I feel a strange pride in hearing this. I wonder if I would have followed through on my suicidal impulse. I'm glad I didn't get the chance to find out. And Mike's spiritual talk gives a boost to my own fledgling positive view of God.

I drop by the Inn and chat with Nick.

"Tony got arrested on the Aurora Bridge last week," he tells me. "And Audrey went into Fairfax, but she's back now. She's much better."

"That's good. Bummer she had to go in."

Then Nick says that Bella is in Harborview right now. I'm shocked. Despite her selective bathing habits, I've always seen her as a solid citizen, someone making her way out of the system.

We go up that evening and visit her in the Harborview psych ward, which is much trashier than Providence. The walls are institutional green and there is lots of clanging and people milling about. As a veteran mental patient, I'm relaxed around all these nut cases—some drugged up, some freaking out, some just acting goofy. We talk with Bella in a cluster of those crummy beige couches that can be found wherever lunatics gather.

She's her familiar, solid self. She says, "Don't worry. I just flipped out on two hits of really bad acid. I'll be out tomorrow and I'll be coming home to the Inn."

I drive Nick back to the halfway house. It's early evening as we pull up and I see the usual group hanging out on the front porch. I check in with Ronnie. He tells me he likes his new therapist, who is helping him ignore his voices.

"He calls the voices 'cowardly personalities'," Ronnie says.

"When I moved in, I was really afraid of you," I tell him.

"Really?" Ronnie seems surprised. "Why?"

"Well, one night I thought you were going to kill me," I tell him.

"Hee hee. I always thought you were going to beat me up," he says.

Audrey looks better than she ever did when I lived here. She's hardly wringing her hands and she's not talking in her whispery voice about germs. She talks in her whispery voice about regular stuff instead. A woman brings the guitar out and sings the Roberta Flack hit, "Killing Me Softly." She sounds pretty good.

I like seeing my former housemates, but I have a different kind of twilight zone sense, one that is bittersweet. I'm fading out of this world and into regular society. As I head down the sidewalk to my car, I glance up at the group on the porch. In the shadows, the chronics sit and tremble. The young people smoke and talk.

I get to walk away.

Joe Guppy, Seattle, 1980.

PART III
POCKETS OF UNFINISHED BUSINESS:
A CLINICAL REVIEW

THE DIALOGUES

More than 30 years ago, a young therapist challenged me with a question: "Are you planning to spend the next 30 years saying, 'Boy, that sure was unfair what happened to me back in 1979'?"

I didn't. But I sure spent the next 30 years profoundly influenced by the events of 1979. As traumatic as the experience was, I emerged from it with purpose and energy.

In early 1980 I reconnected with members of my improvisation class and co-founded a small theater group. The theater was a place where my "weird ideas" could be used for self-expression rather than self-torture. My creative imagination had fueled my paranoia. Now it helped fuel our group's comedy sketches, and surreal improvisations. In the arts community, I didn't have to keep my past a secret; in fact, it gave me street cred.

Theater work led to a career in television. I continued to enjoy writing and performing comedy, but by the mid-nineties, I was ready for a change. I trained to be a psychotherapist at Seattle University's existential-phenomenological psychology master's program. I worked in community mental health for seven years. Then, a few years after opening my private practice in Seattle, I opened my archive box marked "Crazy Period."

When I saw the extent of the materials documenting my story, I envisioned a detailed case study of my journey of spiritual and psychological recovery, which I hoped would be an absorbing narrative on its own but one that also might help people on both sides of the couch.

Several of my contemporary colleagues agreed to discuss my case with me. I also talked with two wonderful people who helped me recover in 1979, Nurse Patricia and Father Carroll. In conversations about everything from Jean-Paul Sartre to the terror bark, we examined my story from a counseling perspective.

ONE: Kurt Dale, LMFT, marriage and family therapist
"We all have this fundamental desire to share... our hell."

TWO: Patricia de la Fuente, LPN, former psychiatric nurse
"You resented it, but thank God, it worked."

THREE: Kevin Devine, MSW, trauma specialist
"We often have pockets of unfinished business."

FOUR: David Goodman, PhD, psychotherapist and teacher
"These things were important to you — so they became important to him."

FIVE: Julia Putnam, MSW, psychotherapist
"Healing is not imposed from on high by the expert..."

SIX: Lane Gerber, PhD, psychotherapist and teacher
"Cripes, I could be that person."

SEVEN: L. Patrick Carroll, former Jesuit priest
"We're not just sitting around, waiting for heaven..."

ONE

"WE ALL HAVE THIS FUNDAMENTAL DESIRE TO SHARE... OUR HELL."

Kurt Dale, LMFT, is a licensed marriage and family therapist with 25 years experience. He has a private practice in Seattle. We talked on a walk around Seattle's Discovery Park.

DALE: You've worked as a psychotherapist for the past 15 years. I'm curious to know—as you look back on your own bout of mental illness—which therapists and which therapeutic methods were most and least helpful to you, and why?

GUPPY: The fundamentals of psychotherapy are affirmed by my experience. It's a cliché to say: "Tell your secrets to your therapist and the truth will set you free," but I'm still amazed by that dramatic moment when I revealed my greatest fear to Dr. Leighter, and it dissolved.

DALE: You mean the time you told Dr. Leighter that you thought you were dead and living in hell?

GUPPY: Yes. I believed that if I told anyone about my fear, the demons would drop the pretense and begin physically torturing me, for all eternity. It takes a tremendous leap of courage to reveal a paranoid delusion. I'm passionate about this in advocating on behalf of other patients. From the outside, we say "it's all in your head," but from the inside, the danger — and thus the courage — are real.

DALE: Why do you think you revealed your fear at that time?

GUPPY: I was exhausted and desperate. I walked into my first session with Dr. Leighter, found him to be steady and empathetic, and spilled my guts. I had no conscious plan to do this. The effect of his therapeutic presence was subliminal. Previously, I had approached this topic with my first psychiatrist, Dr. Hardaway, but I felt like he ignored me.

DALE: You talked about your compelling reasons *not* to share what was going on, but obviously there were also some compelling reasons *to* share.

GUPPY: I did have a hope in a parallel possibility: "Maybe I really AM in a mental hospital." When I told Dr. Leighter my secret he said, "Joe, I don't believe people want to harm you." He didn't try to force anything, he just calmly told me the way he saw things. I took in what he said, left the office, and never was that delusional again. I still sometimes felt paranoid, or had a fear that I was wandering in an unreal twilight zone, but the worst of it — the imminent terror that I was in Satan's Hell — that vanished. Never to return.

DALE: That is amazing. It seems we all have this fundamental desire to tell others what's going on with us, a compelling desire to share our hell with another human being.

GUPPY: I like that: "Share our hell."

DALE: I'm thinking about how long you kept your fears to yourself and developmental theory. When we're children, stuff happens to us, and a lot of us don't talk about it. We can't talk about it. We experience only a "screaming bundle of intolerable pain" as Remarque writes in *All Quiet on the Western Front*.

GUPPY: So a therapist may tell a child, "You can use your words." Or invite the child to use the office sandbox and toys to act out what's going on.

DALE: Then another person can make sense out of our expression. And we are found.

GUPPY: We're seen. Like the infant who sees herself reflected in the gaze of the mother, and therefore knows that she exists as a self, and develops a self in the gaze of the mother. I think we can look at my story in that way—that the psychotic state was so dis-integrating to my reality and to my sense of self that I regressed, not to a complete loss of reality…

DALE: You still had the awareness of others around you, that you were in a room, in a building…

GUPPY: But from a developmental view, the trauma regressed me to that screaming, nonverbal state. I remember coming up out of that and seeing Patricia, the nurse who ended up helping me so much. Subconsciously, it was like "Are you my mother?" I had to rebuild trust and attachment in a very basic way. And she started essentially saying: "Use your words and tell me what happened."

DALE: Like narrative therapy. Which I find works well with children.

GUPPY: Patricia was insistent that I talk about how I got there. I didn't want to go into it, but I'm sure that was essential to regrounding me and in forming a therapeutic relationship with her.

DALE: Why were you reluctant?

GUPPY: I was in a panic state. I was secretly thinking: "Hey, I'm in Hell. What's the point in talking about something that happened before I died?"

DALE: That makes sense.

Both laugh.

DALE: But it's not really that you just didn't think it was relevant. Wasn't there pain or fear in sharing the story with her?

GUPPY: That's not how I remember it. Just that it was a hassle, frustrating, confusing. But I think I'm coming out of denial in this moment as you ask your question. Yes, it *was* painful to tell her my story. But in the longer run it was healing, like scrubbing out a wound. Like a doctor, a therapist needs a good "bedside manner." Patricia had that.

DALE: Maybe she represented what attachment theory would call the good mother, the "good-enough mother."

GUPPY: The notion of Nurse Patricia and Dr. Leighter as mother/father figures is clear to me now but didn't really occur to me at the time. I think of those picky questions I asked Dr. Leighter about water molecules and elevator doors. I think I was rebuilding reality from the ground up, like a four-year-old. Of course, I had a bigger vocabulary, and I referenced modern physics, but it was like the way little kids say, "Daddy, why is the sky blue?"

DALE: I remember that with my kids. You answer one question and there's another one right after it.

GUPPY: The "good-enough" father doesn't lose his patience and say: "Shut up, what's wrong with you?" That was the message I took from Dr. Hardaway. When I asked him about doorknob heights and elevator doors, he said: "What is it inside you that makes you notice those things?" I don't want to be trashing the guy—but wow—doesn't that strike you as an extraordinarily inept response?

DALE: Yes, and it also sounds like what I might see in a training video of a psychiatrist's interaction with a patient. He's asking, "What's that about for *you*?"

GUPPY: If you have a theory as to what he was trying to accomplish clinically with his response, I'd like to hear it.

DALE: It's as if he knows that what you're saying is a metaphor. You're beating around the bush. He's responding: "Use your intelligence. Don't talk to me about doorknobs. What's really going on?"

GUPPY: When you suggest this alternative, the experience softens for me. I know I was paranoid and heard Dr. Hardaway's tone as more sinister than he intended. But Dr. Leighter met me on the more primal, archaic level I was on. He answered my questions literally.

DALE: And he wasn't impatient.

GUPPY: Yes. But sometimes I needed more than just patience to snap me out of my delusional state. The confrontative and cognitive-behavioral techniques often felt like aggressive traps, but confrontation did work when two male nurses physically dragged me out of the elevator during my second escape attempt. That spoke my language. It wasn't intellectual, it was purely physical. It was like: "Welcome to reality. You're not a ghost in some phantom world. We can pull your body down the hall and you can't do anything about it." That woke me up.

DALE: Kick-ass therapy might be a good name for it.

GUPPY: (*Laughs.*) When I worked for an inpatient addiction treatment center, clients in anger management group talked about how the click of the handcuffs, or the slamming of the jail-cell door, woke them up out of their manic, addicted mindset.

DALE: You've painted a pretty glowing picture of Dr. Leighter. What about times when things didn't go so smoothly?

GUPPY: When he cut off my medication, I had a total meltdown. At the time, I was focused on the loss of my mental crutch, but I now realize that, on a deeper level, I felt betrayed. Suddenly, Dr. Leighter was *not* listening, *not* empathizing.

DALE: Which must have been shocking.

GUPPY: Yes. I remember an article about a common narrative arc in psychotherapy: At first, the client idealizes the therapist, but then the therapist makes a mistake and the alliance is broken in some way. So when Dr. Leighter stopped being perfect in my eyes, it was quite the fall.

DALE: That's when he literally turned into a monster?

GUPPY: Yes, that weird perceptual shift.

DALE: But later you were able to repair the relationship?

GUPPY: Yes. And when that happens, the therapeutic relationship comes out even stronger.

DALE: When I think about being with clients when they're in a paranoid or delusional state, I reflect on your insight that, as scary as the delusional world was for you, you sometimes found it preferable to reality.

GUPPY: One time a male nurse I call Terry took us out in the hall for Ping-Pong. I was excited to play, and then I discovered that the medications had taken away my muscle control. On the way back into the ward, Terry seemed to transform into a monster. This was terrifying, but I now believe that subconsciously I was escaping into the drama of my fantasy world. Here's another way delusions served me: My belief that I had already died often led me to dismiss plans of suicide.

DALE: Which might have saved your life.

GUPPY: I think it's crucial that we try to listen for the meaning of many of the seemingly crazy things a client may say and not dismiss them as random neural firings of a diseased brain. That may be the case for some forms of organic brain damage, but I believe most delusions serve a purpose.

DALE: You've talked about being heard and taken seriously, but at another point it was people being firm and literally manhandling you that brought you back to reality.

GUPPY: The overriding factor is the therapist being authentically present. I think of Patricia, one of the most skilled clinicians I encountered. She was like a traveler between worlds. She could join me in my experience and then invite me back into the real world in a firm way, yet leave me with a choice.

DALE: She gave you a strong invitation. I love the image of the mental health professional as a traveler who moves between worlds.

GUPPY: Yes—open, steady, and inviting. I think of that simple
sentence Dr. Leighter often repeated: "I like you, Joe, and
I believe you're going to get better." You can find faith,
hope, and love all right there. "I like you, Joe"—that's
love. "I believe you're going to get better"—that's
faith and hope.

TWO

"YOU RESENTED IT, BUT THANK GOD, IT WORKED."

Patricia de la Fuente, LPN, is a psychiatric nurse, now retired, who was a key to my recovery in 1979. I met with her in her Seattle apartment. First, we collaborated on sketching out, from memory, a floor plan of the hospital's two mental wards. Then I brought out the photocopied nurses' notes from the medical records. She began flipping through the pages and we began our interview.

DE LA FUENTE: Omigosh, I recognize my handwriting. *(She reads her notes.)* "February 7: Joe seems to have better recall and grasp of events leading up to his hospitalization. Today he was able to retrack his time from Seattle to Mexico for a job interview, and back home with parents. Nonetheless he continues to interject: 'Does that sound right to you?'" Yes, I remember you would ask me that.

GUPPY: I felt very shaky and insecure.

DE LA FUENTE: "February 12: Joe does not last long at any one activity. Ping-Pong game lasted five minutes, book reading started and stopped a number of times, he went down to Occupational Therapy and returned after ten minutes."

GUPPY: I remember that jumpy sense of being unable to settle into anything. I attributed that entirely to my own craziness, but in researching my book I learned that there's a side effect of Haldol called "akathisia"—a sense of inner restlessness.

DE LA FUENTE: Sometimes the patients were on way too many medications. That's my own personal opinion.

GUPPY: It's hard to know how much the medications helped and how much they were part of the problem.

DE LA FUENTE: "February 25: Joe entered screaming, escorted by two staff members. He is terribly fearful, suspicious, fears he will surely die, is diaphoretic and some tremors." Your blood pressure was 100 over 50. Fifty is quite low.

GUPPY: That's when I ended up in the security room for the second time.

DE LA FUENTE: I remember. It was very sad. "He clings to nurses' hands, pleading with us, 'Please don't leave me alone.' After 15 minutes calmed down and accepted being poseyed for his protection. Talked with this nurse nonstop for 30 minutes."

GUPPY: I remember waking up with the leather restraint around my waist. I was making that weird barking sound. You asked me, rather bluntly, if I could make a choice to regain control.

DE LA FUENTE: It was an animalistic sound as I recall, Joe. It was quite strange. It was a big concern to us, because a patient who goes into an animalistic sound is clearly not present. They are somewhere else.

GUPPY: I can recall the sound clearly. It was like this: "UNH UNH UNH UNH!" I would do that for a long time.

DE LA FUENTE: The sweating profusely, the dread—that is sheer panic. Some people would use every curse word in the book, some people would scream to God to save them, some people would swear that we were deliberately killing them. The barking sound was your way of expressing it. When that would calm down, I would say to myself, "The medicine is taking hold and he's getting more control." And I would be encouraged.

GUPPY: After I calmed down, I remember getting out of bed and walking up and touching the dark red carpet that was on the walls. That was so bizarre.

DE LA FUENTE: It was a sound-proofing attempt.

GUPPY: At the time I didn't think of that. Or that it would protect me if I threw myself against the wall. I took it as evidence that I had passed over into Hell.

DE LA FUENTE: Yes, and with the dull light it was quite eerie in there. *(Resumes reading.)* This when you start to improve: "March 2: Joe has been more outgoing, sociable, participating in outpatient activities today." I was so happy for you. Do you remember when you first asked me about the piano?

GUPPY: No.

DE LA FUENTE: You asked me, in a sarcastic tone I might add: "Well, I don't suppose you have a piano in this place?" It was a down day for you. And I said, "As a matter of fact we do." So I got special permission from the doctor to take you up there.

GUPPY: I remember sitting at that piano. At first I was so stiff I could barely play, but it got better.

DE LA FUENTE: Well, you played beautifully. And this facial expression would come over you that was so profoundly calming. It speaks of the healing power of the arts.

GUPPY: I notice that my memories of the entire time in the hospital are so soaked in agitation and negativity that it's hard for me to take in what you say. But when I look back from today's perspective, when I look back with compassion, then I recognize that—yes, of course I felt better in those moments at the piano.

DE LA FUENTE: "March 5: Joseph states 'I feel super. It's amazing I really do feel so much better.' Certainly Joe appears calmer, in control, seems to have no tremors. He sounds as though he really wants to trust someone very much. We touched again on Joe's sexual anxieties today, discussed masturbation taboos and guilt."

GUPPY: I was so tangled up with God and guilt and sexuality. I'm glad we could talk about those things. For some reason you and I connected. With the vast majority of the nurses and the doctors, I would be blank and very fearful.

DE LA FUENTE: "March 7: Joe complained of feeling crummy. He went on to say that he still feels pressured by the nurses, including myself..." This actually made me feel good because you trusted me enough to tell me this. You didn't have to cover up how you felt or make it sound more pleasing. *(Resumes reading.)* "April 2: Joe has been up, dressed, to PT and OT and sticking to his daily schedule quite well."

GUPPY: I pasted that schedule into my journal. *(Joe opens up the journal and shows the schedule to Patricia.)*

DE LA FUENTE: My goodness. There it is. "Rise, breakfast, tidy room." It was a challenge to get you to tidy your room. Oh, mother of God, was that a challenge!

GUPPY: We had a battle back and forth about that schedule. I recognize now that I really wanted the structure, but I also resented it and rebelled against it.

DE LA FUENTE: You resented it, but thank God, it worked. Most days it really did.

GUPPY: It did. So what's it been like for you to revisit all this?

DE LA FUENTE: Well, obviously it's been tearful and emotional. It illustrates the great importance of taking individual time with patients and not treating them like numbers.

THREE

"WE OFTEN HAVE POCKETS OF UNFINISHED BUSINESS."

Kevin Devine, MSW (Master's of Social Work) therapist for the Veterans Administration for 12 years, has an interest in both trauma work and altered states of consciousness. Kevin accompanied me when I returned to a building on Seattle's Capitol Hill, the site of my first mental health exam in January 1979. I hadn't been there in more than 30 years, and my only memories of the site were the distorted perceptions I experienced when I returned from Mexico, at the peak of my toxic psychosis.

We are walking toward the building, a few blocks away.

GUPPY: I always used to think my most traumatic moments were when I was freaking out, strapped to my bed in the security ward. But really, the worst was *before* admission, when I was walking around free, paranoid, and experiencing highly distorted perceptions. Sometimes everything in front of me—the walls, people coming toward me—would granulate and fall, like yellow sand. By the time I got to the hospital, even if I thought I was in Hell, at least the walls of Hell had stabilized.

DEVINE: A sense of the visual field being in motion. That's a classic hallucinogenic experience. But your story is more traumatizing than the typical self-induced "bad trip" in that you had no idea you had been dosed. You had no context.

GUPPY: I remember how I perceived the exterior of this building
we are coming up on—it seemed like this surrealistic
architecture, impossible angles, weird, shifting
constructions. M.C. Escher meets Hieronymus Bosch.
Grinding, hanging, mechanical parts. I'm aware that I
have a desire for those perceptions to align somehow
with what I see today. And I want *you* to see what I
see. But I also have this harsh, self-critical thought:
"Who cares? You were hallucinating! Move on!" Why
am I not satisfied to dismiss my memories as a symptom
of insanity? Is that a trauma reaction?

DEVINE: I don't think you have post-traumatic stress disorder,
because you don't have impaired functioning. You've
been able to do what you need to do. But I think a lot
of experiences can have a lasting impact without a
person going into a diagnosable condition. We often have
pockets of unfinished business. You're going back and
penetrating this pocket, trying to rebuild the context,
and wanting to knit it back into the agreed-upon
reality that you and I share.

*We approach the exterior of the building, a Tudor, made of dark,
mottled red brick.*

DEVINE: The overall design of the building has a medieval,
castle-like feeling. It's a creepy building in kind of a
cool way. You could see it as that place where the priest
in *The Exorcist* shows up. Take a look at those
wrought-iron grates on the windows.

GUPPY: Yeah, yeah. Those are definitely original equipment.
Hanging metal parts. My hallucinogenic experiences
usually came with some form of synesthesia, senses
blending together. The visual field is shifting,
everything is shaded blue or yellow, the window
grates are grinding, the inside of my head is grinding
with a whining yellow headache. My inner space is
too connected with the space around me, as if I'm
merged with what I'm seeing, hearing, feeling.

DEVINE: Sounds like what I've read about people with schizophrenia not being able to filter perceptions.

GUPPY: Have you seen the movie *Clean, Shaven*?

DEVINE: Yeah!

GUPPY: When I saw that, I thought: "That's it." Every sound was loud, unfiltered, coming in at the same volume.

DEVINE: Your description is consistent with what I've read in the literature—our brains are exquisitely sensitive, and we have so much sensory stimuli coming in at all times that there are mechanisms built-in to screen stuff out so we can attend to what is important. When you're on a drug or you're having some kind of psychotic experience, those filters are removed or changed. The intensity feels overwhelming.

A plane roars by overhead.

GUPPY: It's like that jet that just went by. Normally, I would filter that out—I wouldn't even hear it. I wonder if we're talking about not only a drug effect, but also that the person is in a fearful, hyper-vigilant state. "I have to know everything that is going on."

DEVINE: You're assessing *everything* as a potential threat.

GUPPY: If you listen to the tape of my later 1979 interview with the social worker, you can hear him make this slight gulping sound, an unusual vocal tic. I perceived it as reverberating loudly through the room. In my hyper-vigilant state, maybe I was acutely attuned to anything that was an anomaly and perceived it as important, big.

DEVINE: That makes sense.

GUPPY: I'm aware that I'm getting what I said I wanted when we started this. You've joined me in investigating this traumatic memory. We've talked about a movie we've both seen where an artist captured part of my experience. It feels good. There's something here about isolation versus community.

DEVINE: With the vast majority of our experiences there is a
sense of connectedness, a logic that gives a sense of
safety in the world, of predictability. You had 20-plus
years of life before this mental break and then 30-plus
years afterwards. For people who experience trauma—
whether it's a tour of duty in war, or an accident, or a
mental break—these are experiences that don't fit.
When you broke from "reality," you felt utterly alone
and disconnected. You were healed, slowly, by re-
establishing a felt sense that others could relate to and
understand what you were experiencing. The need for
that is woven into the fabric of our nature, which is
inherently social.

FOUR

"THESE THINGS WERE IMPORTANT TO YOU–SO THEY BECAME IMPORTANT TO HIM."

David M. Goodman, PhD, is psychotherapist and teacher at Lesley University, Cambridge, and Harvard Medical School.

GUPPY: You wrote a paper responding to a draft version of my book for a psychology seminar at Seattle University a few years back, which you entitled "Clinical De-facing." You contrast some comments that Jean-Paul Sartre made with observations from the philosopher Emmanuel Levinas. Both were talking about the human encounter of the face-to-face.

GOODMAN: Yes. Sartre describes what he calls "the look," which turns a person's experience and very existence into an object of the Looker's gaze. This can be voiced as: "Your perception of me is dangerous to me. Your surveillance of me threatens me, reduces me, and manages me."

GUPPY: And you see elements of this in my encounters with my first psychiatrist, Dr. Hardaway.

GOODMAN: You write: "He [Dr. Hardaway] cuts off my ramblings and announces it's time for a physical exam. I meekly comply, but as Satan comes at me with his stethoscope, I'm terrified this is the start of the physical torture." Perhaps even in his approach, in his questions, in his gaze, the torture had already started. I frequently hear patients who are not in a psychotic state like you were complain about their medication management appointments. The clinician sits behind a computer, asking prepackaged questions, typing away. Covering predesignated terrain. The patient is not allowed to be truly Other.

GUPPY: Yes. As a therapist, I think Levinas' idea of respecting the client's "otherness" is key. That's why we ask open-ended, non-assumptive questions. Not: "That must have been awful! I know just how you feel," but rather: "What was that like for you?"

GOODMAN: Your second psychiatrist, Dr. Leighter, seemed to respond much better to what Levinas describes as the "demand" the Other makes upon us in the face-to-face. He listened, attended, and responded. He didn't pre-conceptualize theories as to why you were asking about the height of the ceiling or the make-up of the elevator doors. These things were important to you — so they became important to him. It is a joining and a "living with" that allows an opening into something expansive and new and healing.

GUPPY: When you speak of the notion of the "demand of the face of the Other," I think of that striking example Dr. George Kunz cites of the Nazi guards who defended their actions by saying "I was only following orders." Levinas says that the face of the Other gives a countermanding order, "Do not do violence to me." Oops—I just realized I don't want to be comparing my experience to that of a prisoner in a Nazi concentration camp.

GOODMAN: Of course not, but Levinas did recognize that not all violence is physical. There is the violence of being "totalized" by language, by scientistic reductionism, or by one-size-fits-all manual-driven therapies. I fear this is the direction that institutional mental health treatment moves toward.

GUPPY: You wrote that my experience with the nurse Melba was one of those "mundane inter-human exchanges where the Divine is invited to pass, where healing and transformation ambulates." Tell me more about that.

GOODMAN: I was struck by your description of making the bed with Melba: "working slowly alongside her, I sometimes briefly feel like an ordinary person doing an ordinary thing." So often, even the best therapeutic training urges us to look for the grand aha moment, the sensationalized insight.

GUPPY: Like in *Good Will Hunting* when Robin Williams tells Matt Damon "It's not your fault."

GOODMAN: Exactly. This can be yet another way that we de-face our patients by seeking impact, by grasping for a heroic Hollywood moment.

GUPPY: Your phrase "where the Divine is invited to pass," reminds me of the Levinasian elements of my own encounter with the Divine, when I was strapped to my hospital bed. I had the sense not merely that this divine presence exists, but that the presence was perceiving *me*, looking at me, with understanding and compassion.

FIVE

"HEALING IS NOT IMPOSED FROM ON HIGH BY THE EXPERT..."

Julia Putnam, MSW, LICSW, began working in the mental health field at a Pacific Northwest residential treatment center in 1974. I met with her in her psychotherapy office in Seattle.

GUPPY: You're familiar with the different therapy styles I encountered at the time of my hospitalization in 1979. I'm particularly interested in the sometimes hostile "confrontative" style, which is still used today by TV talk show therapists and others. What do you know about its history?

PUTNAM: It came into therapeutic fashion in the 1960s and 1970s, a reaction to the "gray flannel suit, button-down" psychiatry of the 1950s, in which the psychiatrist maintained a distant, blank-slate persona.

GUPPY: In the hospital, the younger generation of therapists used the confrontative style, whereas, with one exception, every psychiatrist I encountered seemed cold, distant, even robotic. Do you know how *that* style came about?

PUTNAM: It developed out of the Second World War. Troubled veterans were returning from the war. There wasn't much prior understanding of PTSD, but people knew *something* was going on, so there was great interest in psychology and psychiatry. Also, there was a push to get women out of doing the "Rosie the Riveter" thing and back into traditional roles. Psychiatry and psychology became the voice of stability and authority, the voice of assurance: "We know the right way to do things; we have the answers."

GUPPY: I wonder if that relates to the dominance of the nuclear bomb at the end of World War II. Science provided the answer to the war; psychiatry also became scientific and authoritative. We solve problems with mathematics and linear logic, including problems of the human psyche.

PUTNAM: I understand Freud was convinced of his own scientific authority, having come out of neurology.

GUPPY: A psychoanalyst I talked with, who was trained in the early 1960s, pointed out that the cold and distant attitude I encountered was like that of the observing scientist, the surgeon who doesn't want to "contaminate the operating room." In this case, the contamination would be any content coming from the therapist, or even his presence.

PUTNAM: There was the belief that you could somehow avoid that. Exhibiting courtesy and warmth was considered intruding yourself into the scientific observables.

GUPPY: So the sixties came along in rebellion to this, questioning authority, questioning Western science. And out of that arose confrontative therapy.

PUTNAM: I believe the technique was pioneered by groups like Synanon and EST.

GUPPY: Synanon being the drug treatment program and EST the self-help movement founded by Werner Erhard. How would you describe this approach?

PUTNAM: It utilized direct challenges to the patient and paradox—"in your face."

GUPPY: Which is the therapist explicitly *not* staying distant, *not* staying out of the patient's space. A therapist at Seattle Mental Health I call Alvin said to me in group: "You're whining. You expect me to tell you what to do? Maybe you think I'm going to grow boobs so you can suck on my tit?" It felt like verbal shock therapy.

PUTNAM: Where I worked, it wasn't required that we use the confrontative style. It was something the "cool kids" would try.

GUPPY: So you didn't use it?

PUTNAM: No.

GUPPY: Why not?

PUTNAM: Something about it didn't seem right, or didn't seem suited to who I was. It was often practiced impulsively, which seemed to end up being more about the therapist's own frustrations, concerns, and fears.

GUPPY: The justification for it might be: "This is the impulse that is coming up for me right now—so let it all hang out." A counterculture reaction to the "uptight establishment."

PUTNAM: Yes. "This is what I'm feeling right now, so I'll go ahead and say it."

GUPPY: At that time I would have idealized the "hippie era" as a great leap forward for freedom. But in this case, the freewheeling style felt like an attack. There was a smarmy, smirking quality.

PUTNAM: Like they had your number. And they were letting you know it.

GUPPY: I was always accused of being manipulative and not taking responsibility. Now I'm sure I *was* passive-aggressive and evasive, but this just made me feel bad about myself.

PUTNAM: That's an oddity of the human potential movement, like EST—the harsh, karmic stuff. It was saying you are responsible for your reality, meaning you could be in control, which is an illusion.

GUPPY: There was another therapist at Seattle Mental Health, whom I call Lars, who practiced with a confrontative style but who was extremely helpful. When Alvin led the group, there was palpable tension, but Lars had a warm, attentive presence, even when he was challenging us.

PUTNAM: It sounds like he was also practicing empathy and compassion, so those elements informed your overriding experience of him. His focus was on your welfare.

GUPPY: Yes, Lars could be abrupt and blunt, but he never used direct sarcasm.

PUTNAM: Which has a demeaning edge. I think the distinction is: Lars was not acting out his own need. It's easy to flip over into that when doing these techniques. It's a fine line.

GUPPY: But that style isn't just an artifact of the sixties and seventies. It's still popular, at least on TV shows like *Dr. Phil.*

PUTNAM: They practice the "snap out of it" school of therapy.

GUPPY: A few years ago, I saw a TV therapist accuse a woman of not showing enough gratitude for all the expensive experts he had brought in to try to help her.

PUTNAM: Sounds like he may have been fulfilling his own need to be praised.

GUPPY: The other technique I encountered in the hospital was cognitive-behavioral therapy (CBT). It may have been helpful to other patients, but for me it was a mismatch. Here's a copy of a handout I was given.

PUTNAM: *(Reading.)* "The Problem Solving Process and You." Yes, this looks very familiar. The typewriting is so evocative of the time. An IBM Selectric.

GUPPY: I didn't tell them what was going on in my mind, so they had no way of knowing what a mental thumbscrew this was for me. But I was operating in a mythical arena, wrestling with demons and eternal damnation, while they were asking me to engage at a much higher cognitive level. I interpreted all these points and sub-points, which march through an inescapable, logical system, as part of my punishment.

PUTNAM: There was a textbook at the time, written by two behaviorists named Ullman and Krasner, which described absolutely everything in behavioral terms, including thought disorder. I see that as almost dismissing your experience, saying, "We are going to define the world in a certain way, and we insist that you live in it."

GUPPY: I'm concerned that today there is a strong movement for "cognitive-behavioral fits all." It's supposedly "evidence-based," while talk therapy is considered vague and unscientific. There is more evidence for math than poetry, but the poetry of human relationship may be more crucial to healing than the math of sophisticated psychological technique.

PUTNAM: I like that very much. For those of us who have been in the business a long time, we see therapists get enamored of different techniques, and then a kind of religiosity sets in, and it becomes about the book, the manual, the way you're supposed to do it.

GUPPY: Even though multiple studies have shown that, regardless of the technique, the relationship between the client and therapist is primary.

PUTNAM: I would point out that whatever the technique, you've noted that the therapist was helpful if he or she seemed to be working on your behalf and was warm and empathetic. Healing is not imposed from on high by the expert and his methods; rather, the capacity for self-healing is within the person.

SIX

"CRIPES, I COULD BE THAT PERSON."

Lane Gerber, PhD, is a clinical psychologist, professor emeritus at Seattle University, and a former teacher of mine in graduate school. We met in his home in north Seattle.

GUPPY: I'm thinking about when I lived in the halfway house and about my relationships with my housemates there. The therapists would tell us that the halfway house with the treatment center across the street was a "therapeutic milieu." I thought this sounded like bullshit, but it actually ended up working that way, without me even being aware of it. I did go through some sort of healing process—I started out there very isolated, seeing my housemates as demons and zombies.

GERBER: You were scared. Your roommate seems like he's threatening to kill you...? I know that would have freaked me out.

GUPPY: Yeah, but then I start to see him more clearly. I talked to Nick about him and found out he sniffed paint. When I came out of my twilight zone state, Ronnie seemed more like a nut case than a demon, but I was still scared. And then when I started talking with him my perspective shifted again. I realized that he wasn't threatening me. He was having some bizarre conversation with his voices.

GERBER: So now he's this guy who's trying to live with his voices.

GUPPY: Yeah.

GERBER: And that's a bitch for him. So he's become a person. He's not the monster anymore. He's not the really crazy guy. He's… he's Ronnie. You even come to the point where you can tell him, "Knock it off, you're keeping me awake."

GUPPY: A more trusting level.

GERBER: A much more trusting level. Crazy has some of its power taken away in these little interactions, your moment-to-moment movements toward seeing the other patients as people.

GUPPY: These connections I felt with Ronnie, Ken, Nick, and Bella, they were like flowers coming up through the cracks in the concrete in a prison. We didn't just hunker down for our own bare survival. This human-to-human kindness blossomed even under those dismal conditions.

GERBER: Maybe you *are* like prisoners in this place. Maybe because of the broken-down living space you've been assigned, it's like society has thrown you away. And the distinctions among you don't matter anymore. You're getting down to something realer than that.

GUPPY: Then it goes to another level. I not only want to feel safe with my housemates, I actively want to help them. This is not anything I thought about or tried to do. It just happened. I end up feeling protective of Ronnie, like he's my little brother. And I follow after Ken when he walks out of group, knowing that he was in danger of losing his housing.

GERBER: You didn't want that to happen to one of your fellow prisoners. You know things may not be great now, but they could get *really* bad. You've become part of the group, and the group's become part of you. And then somehow you take some of the power of

just being a person and go out and say to Ken, "Hey,
it's okay. You can keep it together for a little while."

GUPPY: It's like we were buddies in a war zone, veterans of
the hospital wars, the mental health war. Maybe we
felt the rest of society was at war with us. So you're
called to help a buddy. The therapists would tell us
that the halfway house is halfway *up* to getting back
to normal life. But they also made it clear that the Inn
was temporary housing, so you might be on your way
back *down*. You're halfway down to the street, halfway
to the forgotten wards of Western State hospital,
halfway to the Aurora Bridge. When I was talking to
Ken, trying to get him back into group, we both knew
what was at stake.

GERBER: I think Washington State is something like 48th in
the nation in psychiatric beds. Society has said, "These
people aren't people anymore."

GUPPY: There's a mental health halfway house near where I
work. I walk by there from time to time and I can look
over at the residents with two sets of eyes. I can see them
the way I imagine the average citizen might, "Whoa, I'm
glad those people are warehoused over there. Look at
that weird guy shaking, that woman staring off into
space. Bunch of wackos." Or, having been one of those
wackos myself, I can think about what kind of healing
might be taking place there, what kind of true social
interactions, true friendships, are happening in that
community. Right now I feel very sad. I know mental
illness is something that has vexed humankind for
millennia, but we could do better, starting with this
idea of the human person—not dismissing people.

GERBER: For all our bravado, we get scared really quickly.
We get scared mental illness is contagious. We don't
want to see it. Because we feel at some level, if we
start down that path, what's going to happen to us?
Do you think anybody will care? Think the world will
care? Doubtful.

GUPPY: What do you mean "if we start down that path"?

GERBER: If we look and allow ourselves the thought that, "Cripes, I could be that person."

GUPPY: Yes.

GERBER: "Oh no, not me."

GUPPY: So in order to see the Other as a human person, you have to identify with the Other in some way. If you block them off as a separate category over there—not human—then that's a lot safer. But if I say they *are* human, now we're getting closer to the idea that I could be like that. When people are asked "What's your greatest fear?" they always say spiders or snakes or heights. No one wants to talk about the greatest fear of all: insanity. We are afraid when we hear the screams of the mentally ill. If we go up to the door of madness and knock, and ask "What's going on in there?" we're afraid we'll be sucked in.

GERBER: We'll be grabbed right in. We don't want to be that different. Because if we are that different, we might not be seen as part of the human community anymore. Your story has such power to it, such down-to-earth realness. You're not writing about your experience in a crazy place with crazy people. You're one of them, and in a sense we're all one of them.

GUPPY: Well, I'm certainly grateful for those people who weren't afraid to knock on my door.

SEVEN

"WE'RE NOT JUST SITTING AROUND, WAITING FOR HEAVEN..."

Pat Carroll was a Jesuit for more than 40 years and was crucial in helping me work through the spiritual turmoil that plagued me during this adventure. He is currently married and living in Seattle. We met at his apartment.

GUPPY: In an email you said you were struck by my "religious experiences, which are nearly universal but rarely spoken of, so rarely trusted."

CARROLL: Yes. For many years, I've organized groups and collected stories to encourage people to talk about their relationship with "God" or "the Transcendent" or whatever they call it. Not necessarily religious but spiritual.

GUPPY: We hear a lot about the "stigma of mental illness," but do you think there's also a stigma in talking about spiritual experience?

CARROLL: If you don't talk about it and find out that other people have similar experiences, you don't trust it.

GUPPY: Two stories that have helped me trust my experience are one from Bill Wilson, the founder of Alcoholics Anonymous, and one from Martin Luther King. Bill Wilson also sensed God as some sort of manifestation of light while he was in the hospital. And MLK speaks about getting a death threat on his bedroom phone late one night. He goes downstairs and, sitting in his kitchen, he hears an inner voice of the Holy Spirit saying: "I'm with you. I'm here with you." A message almost identical to the one I heard. I figure if Bill Wilson or MLK can have these "crazy" spiritual experiences, maybe it's okay for me, too.

CARROLL: I've seen literally hundreds of these types of experiences and I could tell you two or three of my own.

GUPPY: Tell me one of your own.

CARROLL: Around 1972, my dad was dying, and I was the president of a Jesuit high school and the superior of the religious community, even though I was the youngest priest. I was in way over my head. One night, after an awful community meeting, I escaped—I drove 20 miles to Seattle to see some friends. I only got about an hour of sleep because I had to say Mass in the morning. After Mass, I went into my office, feeling like a failure and the biggest fake in the history of the world. I'm sitting there—hating myself and my job—and the sun came up directly behind Mount Rainier. It shone over the mountain and flooded into my office. I had this overwhelming sense of God's presence telling me: "Pat, I love you and you can't stop me."

GUPPY: Nice.

CARROLL: It changed my life. Even though I was professionally religious, I had never had an experience like that. I wasn't looking for it, but I sure needed it. Because of that experience, I have been able to listen for it in others.

GUPPY: I know that empathy is a component of your spiritual counseling, not just in your attitude toward me, but in the scriptures you pointed out to me. You said: "Jesus felt the same way" or "Paul had a similar struggle."

CARROLL: I think the heart of Christian mythology is about the empathy of God, of God wanting to pitch his tent next to ours, to stand alongside us and know our fears and our joys. That's why I believe in—"believe in" is a funny phrase—that is why I *live out of* the Jesus story—whether it's "true" or not. I think a good Buddhist can be as happy as a good Christian, but the Jesus myth works for me because it says God is very close and walks along with us and wanted to be one of us.

GUPPY: I'm thinking of two ways of looking at Jesus on the cross. As a kid, there was that bloody, life-size crucified Christ on the wall of St. Joseph's church. It seemed so frightening and bizarre.

CARROLL: Anyone who grew up with that is haunted by it.

GUPPY: I don't think it's appropriate for kids—they can't get their mind around it. And we were taught that *we* put the nails in his hands...

CARROLL: That kind of focus misses the whole point of the passion story.

GUPPY: Instead, I like the concept that our own trials are like our own crucifixions and that Jesus felt the same way I do sometimes: forsaken and hopeless. He's getting through it because he claims a connection with a higher power, and maybe I can have a similar connection that will get me through.

CARROLL: And he trusts that if he's faithful and acts out of what he believes, God will be faithful. The Christian story is that God is faithful and that life comes out of death. The only reason you can believe in resurrection at the end of your life is that you experience it as you go along, new life coming out of the "deaths" you experience. Joe Guppy is a much better person at 33, 43, 53 than he was at 23 because of what he went through. We're not just sitting around, waiting for heaven, waiting for "pie in the sky when you die." (*Pauses.*) You emailed me this: "An atheist friend once asked: 'You now believe that your perception of Dr.

Hardaway as Satan and your fear of demons were delusions. But why do you consider your mystical encounter with God to be real?'" It's a great question.

GUPPY: A reader could conclude that I just chose the more pleasant delusion. I'm fine with that. But there are some differences.

CARROLL: Some crazy people are spiritually delusional in a really grandiose way. They think they're the Messiah, that God's on their side, that they can step in front of trains or jump off buildings and survive. I wouldn't trust those experiences.

GUPPY: There was a period when I was convinced I could walk through the hospital walls if I wanted to. But that didn't feel like it came from God. It was the fruits of desperate suicidality—"I can't stand being here, so I need to perceive reality as evanescent." In my authentic God experiences, there was drama but also serenity, peace, and calm. I felt grounded in reality during, and after, the experience.

CARROLL: The fruits of the spirit are joy, peace, patience, kindness. Saint Ignatius talked about "consolation without cause" as one of the primary signs of the spirit. You're going through life, you're not doing anything different, and then you're overwhelmed by consolation, you feel warm or comforted or loved. That's how God acts.

GUPPY: That matches my experience. My sense of spiritual connection stayed with me as I became sane, whereas the paranoia faded away.

CARROLL: Have you ever thought—what if you hadn't taken the medication during your Mexico trip that sent you over the edge?

GUPPY: I think if I hadn't taken it, I would have suffered along as neurotic and I wouldn't have had to look so deeply at my many insecurities and fears. If my experience was a gift, it was a crash course in "You need to get it together around your relationships with women, around your religious fears, issues with Dad, etc." Don't get me wrong—I still had plenty of problems yet to face in those areas—but this experience knocked me way ahead of where I would have been without it.

CARROLL: So it was almost a blessing.

GUPPY: Absolutely. I wouldn't claim that there is a divine mastermind that specifically plans everything that happens to us. That doesn't take into account human freedom, or chance, or the fact that there's a lot of mystery in life. But I do believe that God makes a promise that *whatever* happens to us can ultimately work out for the good.

CARROLL: It's a very affirming story. I pray that the story of your healing can be a source of hope to others. That's the best reason for writing it.

ACKNOWLEDGMENTS

I would like to thank the vast number of people who supported me with this project, knowing I will inevitably leave out someone important. First and foremost: my wife Nancy Guppy. Hans Altwies, Dave Baab, Lynne Baab, Mike Baab, Anne Baumgartner, Dan Baumgartner, Jesse Baumgartner, David Brotherton, Lyall Bush, David Byrd, Pete Cannon, Pat Carroll, Lesli Corthell, Charles Cross, Kurt Dale, Brangien Davis, Patricia de la Fuente, Kevin Devine, Ed Durgan, Jerry Evergreen, Phyllis Fletcher, Greg Fritzberg, Tim Gabor, Lane Gerber, David Goodman, Mark Guppy, Paul Guppy, Pauline Guppy, Tim Guppy, Steen Halling, Jim Harbaugh, Chris Harmon, Bev and Alden Harris, Teri Hein, Charles Huffine, Hugo House, Jane Kaplan, John Kazanjian, Kevin Krycka, Greg Kucera, George Kunz, Stephanie Lawyer, B. Frayn Masters, John Maulding, Brian McDonald, Joel McHale, Sheila Mullen, Bob Nelson, Pauline Theo Nestor, Bruce Oberg, Kathleen Pape, Linas Phillips, Julia Putnam, Susan Roberts, Roberta Brown Root, Jan Rowe, Joanna Ryan, Kevin Sampsell, George Sayre, Sebastien Scandiuzzi, Seattle University Masters in Psychology program, Matt Smith, Daniel Spils, Annie St. John, Amy Thone, Bob Tischler, Annette Toutonghi, Jeff Weatherford, Lauren Weedman, John Lawrence Wilson, Jeannie Yandel, my editors Meredith Maran and Karin Snelson, my publisher Ken Shear.

RECOMMENDED BOOKS

PSYCHOLOGY/ PHILOSOPHY:

Frankl, Viktor E. *Man's Search for Meaning*. Boston: Beacon, 1959.

Gendlin, Eugene T. *Focusing*. New York: Bantam, 1978.

Havens, Leston L. *A Safe Place*. New York: Ballantine, 1991.

Kunz, George. *The Paradox of Power and Weakness: Levinas and an Alternative Paradigm for Psychology*. Albany: State University of New York, 1998.

Merleau-Ponty, Maurice. *The Primacy of Perception*. Evanston: Northwestern University Press, 1964

Van Den Berg, J. H. *A Different Existence: Principles of Phenomenological Psychopathology*. Pittsburgh: Duquesne UP, 1972.

Yalom, Irvin D. *Love's Executioner and Other Tales of Psychotherapy*. London: Penguin, 1989.

MEMOIR:

Grealy, Lucy. *Autobiography of a Face*. Boston: Houghton Mifflin, 1994.

Kaysen, Susanna. *Girl, Interrupted*. New York: Vintage, 1994.

McCall, Nathan. *Makes Me Wanna Holler: A Young Black Man in America*. New York: Vintage, 1995

Rogers, Annie G. *A Shining Affliction: A Story of Harm and Healing in Psychotherapy*. New York, NY, Viking, 1995.

Sacks, Oliver W. *A Leg to Stand On*. New York: Summit, 1984.

Vonnegut, Mark. *The Eden Express*. New York: Praeger, 1975.

Wolff, Tobias. *In Pharaoh's Army: Memories of the Lost War*. New York: Knopf, 1994.

ABOUT THE AUTHOR

Seattle native Joe Guppy, an award-winning writer and performer, worked in theater and television from 1980 to 1995. In 1996, he switched careers and trained to be a psychotherapist at Seattle University's existential-phenomenological master's program. He was a community mental health counselor for seven years and currently has a private practice in Seattle. Visit his websites at www.joeguppy.com and www.joeguppywriter.com.

Discover more books and learn about our
new approach to publishing at **booktrope.com**.